THE BLITZ BOY

II

Politics and Invention

Throughout the 1900s

TERRY FITZGERALD

PROLOGUE

Unlike my first book this is not about me and my life but it is intended to reflect the ways and times of the 20th century. I think that particularly regarding politics I will perhaps occasionally stray into the early 21st century.

I've decided to divide it into two books, the first will track the political progression based on what I have learnt, first from my parents and then from my personal observations and sharing opinions with fellow workers, drinkers, and club members.

I will comment on the positive and negative nature as I feel fit but will say here that most of the Political Progression was for short-term and personal career progression. The second book will reflect Natural Progression which I see as invention, innovation, mechanical and medicinal discovery and usage. This is generally more positive and has given many worthwhile and lasting improvements to life.

The chapters and subheadings are not exclusive and where over-lapping occurs I might feel the need to be repetitious. Some chapters may appear to automatically fit into a previous chapter but are treated separately for either their importance or significance; for example Unions, NHS, Post Office, National Service etc.

I hope you read this in the context of a serious reflection on the 1900s but recognise that it is a snapshot of how I perceive that time through my eyes and that it is an opinion and not a criticism. We cannot turn the clock back but should look forward to the future in the knowledge that the past has not failed us.

PART ONE

POLITICAL PROGRESSION

In order for you to follow the progression through the chapters I would like you to understand that my thinking pattern first addresses Central Government generally referring to what it does year after year. All the actions each year have limited or significant impact on the future. After discussing these processes I then move on to Local Government before discussing individually the most significant changes implemented during the 1900s. As these changes impact existing as well as new ideas I have in a number of cases included an element of history.

CHAPTERS

CHAPTER ONE

CENTRAL GOVERNMENT

A POTTED HISTORY

The government as I understand is made up from two democracies, the national election (which elects a party to govern on a first past the post basis) and then the Parliament which debates and passes laws and votes them through, where they are then passed to the upper house, for ratification and or amendment and then written into law by the civil servants before finally being passed into law via Royal approval.

The basis of this kind of parliament developed through many decades and became stable and respected well before my story begins.

In the early part of the 19th century the Members of Parliament were more moral vocationalists and were made up of ex professionals, businessmen and respected citizens. This however, especially after the Second World War changed and being an M P became a profession, as nowadays you can obtain a degree in politics and make it a career. It was also common in forties and fifties to see when the party in power had only a small majority that MP's would be brought in to the chamber from their sick beds in order to see the vote got passed. This all changed later when the speaker agreed to a vote to arrange pairing. This was specifically to help cope with modern travel where MP's began to attend global meetings and would have been unable to vote while away on official business. It later became the norm for a member of any party to request a member of the party in power to pair with them on almost any pretext.

The other side to the history of parliament is the role of the Civil Service. This is derived from the real meaning of servant and they were there to support the requests of the politicians and to also protect them from themselves by making sure their missives were worded clearly and in good legalese. Somewhat like an old fashioned management secretary looked after her boss. The process has developed and changed many times and has sometimes been interpreted by the Civil Servants as if they were the policy and lawmakers. Overall the system has always worked and if the process was not clearly what was intended this was usually corrected by the courts and amended by precedent. More recently with the politician becoming a professional and having his/her own Public Relations department an element of schism has sometimes evolved and all three (MP, Civil Servant and Judge) have at times tried to alter the original intention into their own personal interpretation of what they feel would support their visions for the future.

CHAPTER TWO

SOCIAL IMPACT

AS I SEE IT.

Let me start with the first half of the century which is where I rely on hearsay but I believe that the founding of the Labour Party, the Suffragettes and the General Strike influenced the governments of the day to respond to create laws to benefit and protect the working class and standing of women in their daily life. Examples of this would be:

The introduction of pension's provision.

Better working conditions (better working hours and provision of toilets etc.).

Keeping children for reward and not being allowed to encourage children into seduction or prostitution.

Provision of school meals.

Motor traffic law for rules of the road, cab fares regulating cab meters and collecting road funds.

The Allotment act.

Allowing women to enter Parliament.

The trade Union Act.

Town and Country Planning Act which included compulsory purchase invested in local councils and commitment to create housing (possibly the start of Local Council Housing).

Introduction of a Post Office ministry and the British Broadcasting Corporation (BBC).

Creation of the Utilities Companies

Introduction of National Service.

Education Act 1944 (Primary and secondary education and the related 11 plus exam).

As a child at this time living in a Council House and having working class parents, Dad working three day shifts and a Saturday night, I did feel that people were interested in voting and the various Parties rented High Street shops as committee rooms from which to run their Election campaigns.

The second half (i.e. after the Second World War) is more of my era and as we recovered from food rationing and the ravages of the bombing the National Health Service was introduced. This I think was the last time one felt that the government was actually listening directly to the needs of the people before the professional changes started to appear.

Since then in no particular order this is my view.

The Channel Tunnel should have been two tunnels which I think was one of the early proposals and would have given greater benefits to both France and the U K.

Along with the tunnel it was proposed to build a motorway from Folkestone to Honiton. This was too simplistic and appeared to be one of those ideas that was meant to collect votes from the West Country. A much more positive plan would have been a super highway that only went as far as Southampton and this would have serviced the proposed container port alongside the current port, which was in the pipeline. This proposal was scrapped by a later parliament and replaced with a container port at Felixstowe with links to Liverpool and Manchester. The Southampton idea could have taken advantage of the twin tides and enabled more traffic to be handled. This could also have encouraged long distance lorry drivers to travel from Eastern Europe in modern container-lorries with sleeping facilities (surely a major benefit to the whole of Europe) and clearly less transferring of containers at extra ports and simpler customs controls. When they cancelled the Southampton container port they also cancelled all planned and approved highways developments. The result of this is that many small towns and villages are still blocked with major traffic instead of being by-passed.

If the by-passes had been built there is a distinct possibility that there would not have been a need to consider a high speed rail link from south to north or east to west. They did however spend fortunes on these rail proposals before they were fully passed in government, which meant when the whole thing was appearing to get out of hand it was claimed that having spent so much money to date we must accept the escalating costs to justify the past lack of control. The north south HS1 and HS2 were I believe a political decision to try any grab the northern votes by selling the idea that we could re-industrialise the north.

Somewhere along the way in the 60s and 70s starting with Edward Heath we joined a common market, which turned out not to a simple market but a political unification and morphed into the European Union which was intended to become the equivalent of the Federal states of America but to be more effective. This struggled to grow quickly and the U K were destined to consider exiting.

In the long run it was this exiting (Brexit) that achieved the change in the voting pattern.

Airport expansion is another area where I feel it would have been better to pass this on to the entrepreneurs and let it be decided on enterprise for action and funds. The question that should have been addressed by the politicians was as to whether a new airport would be needed in say a further fifty years.

Soon after the Second World War lobbying of politicians within the parliament chambers was permitted and this led to minority groups getting a vastly over proportionate hearing next to the wheels of power. A major demand was the perceived need for total equality of the sexes, which appears a fair and obvious aim, was loaded with a significant bias and many demands resulted in the law of unintentional consequences. Examples of this are single mothers getting things like housing benefit in their own right while having no intention of ever going out to work. When benefits were introduced, the original idea appeared to be that you paid your stamp and then you earned certain benefits, e.g. sick pay. Sick pay used only to click in after three working days had been lost and needed a medical certification from your GP.

This became self-certificated and could not be readily seen as always honest. Divorce became absorbed in this need for equality and the courts interpreted the new laws so that instead of being allowed to proportion the split on a clear understanding of the circumstances they started to split all monies including personal pensions and investments, including the house, as near as possible equally. The richer people did manage to take the courts on and get variations based on length of the partnership and input, including giving up work to parent the children.

With a new zest for government to get their teeth into more of the everyday life we were introduced to, Health and Safety, Regional Councils, Financial Control, and Audit Control requiring Company Boards to be legally bound to certain accounting restrictions and commitments to providing more holidays and time off for child care and visits to dentists etc.

This bred the growth of quangos who along with Local government Bodies were to be allowed legal status to fine people and companies for not fulfilling various actions or standards. All this led to all of the Utility companies and other critical groups like schools being monitored by non- elected bodies paid fortunes to create a certain level of havoc. Most of these Quangos had their own personal agendas and I am not sure parents had any say in the raising of the school leaving age from 16 to 18 or in the changing of Technical colleges into Universities and then attempting to get 80 plus per cent of school leavers to attend university. This was apparently on an assumption that a university degree guaranteed a more affluent future for both the student and the Country. Unfortunately most things in life reduce to a lowest common denominator and not the highest. Currently the difference between earnings five years after graduation is now as little as 10 to 20 per cent over ordinary school leavers.

Another area that suffered the result of unintentional consequences was the drive, mainly by DoGooders for multiculturalism when what it was probably meant to introduce was inclusion into the society. Inclusion could have had a racist translation and did not take off and multicultural got translated for the worse.

Another major change in attitudes, which may or may not have evolved directly from government but again evolved from the unintended consequences theory, is the compensation Society where everyone feels that everything in life should be perfect and that they have a right to be compensated if they feel standards fall short. This seems to have derived from the passing of Human Rights law. The court of Human Rights started in England but subsumed into European Law at a higher level than England's highest court. It would appear that everybody obtained a right but they themselves also were relieved of responsibility and no individual or Business concern could make a genuine error.

This has been an attempt to show social impact as an evolution of specific actions. In the next section I will discuss specific actions under defined headings and mention positive, negative and consequential outcomes. It is hoped that this taster will encourage you to read on.

CHAPTER THREE

NATIONAL SERVICE

National Service, where do you begin! This from my memory came in almost immediately after the Second World War but I do not know why or for what particular purpose. It could have been for many reasons. There may have been such pressure on getting the men back from war into the workplace and it was felt that it would be a good thing to be educating and training the young men that had not had a father at home for many years was a good way of going forward and not saturating the workplace with cheap labour. Whatever it was in the early days most people saw it a particularly beneficial and it did seem that the boys signed up or were enlisted for a minimum of two years started out as boys and returned home as men.

The significant downside was both the Suez and Korean wars which claimed the lives of a number of 'our' boys. The plus side was that many young men came out skilled or semi-skilled to work in a trade and all had learnt what a real day's work was.

Not all that long before they actually decided to abolish this Service the lobbying began and a small group of people thinking they were doing their best for the lads argued that as they could go to war and die for their Country they should be treated as men and therefore the age of majority which was twenty one should be dropped to 18 years old. I could not understand this as they only appeared to be men after National Service not before. My view was not the perceived one and the age of majority was changed to 18. No real problem but!

The unions got involved in the pay of these young men and pressed for them to be paid a full man's wage at the age of 18. Costly but no obvious problem except that now the traditional apprenticeship of usually five years from the age of 16 to 21 and the first learning years in Insurance, Accounting and Banking etc. with progressive increases in wages over each of the 5 years, now, after only three years employers had to pay a full wage to a trainee.

So was National Service a good thing? Yes it did an excellent job and was possibly stopped too soon. Should we bring back National Service? It would be very difficult but not necessarily a bad thing to consider. We have now got an educational gap of potentially two years for the less academic where they appear to be in limbo. This could be filled by bringing back traditional trade apprenticeships where the trades themselves provide all the resources from the workplace, that is, on the job training and education. This could avoid job seeker allowance before the youngsters had even found a job or even learnt what a working life entails. Who would we then want to enlist into the armed forces if we now have a good take up in both university entry and apprenticeships. Again not an easy question to answer but if we returned the age of majority to 21 we could, if there still appeared to be a problem transferring from education to the workplace slip in a short period of National Service at that point.

CHAPTER FOUR

NATIONALISATION

Is nationalisation a good thing? Well the idea was around in the early 1900's and it would appear that an early participant was the BBC in 1926 but the whole idea took off in the Labour Party manifesto in 1945. The manifesto described why they believed it was necessary for the country going forward. Having been elected they got on with the job. All the major utilities were targeted and these were generally Coal, Gas, Electricity, Water and Communications with Iron and Steel left for a couple of years.

The main drift of the argument was that these industries were not being run well enough and that the government could and would do a better job.

I am not convinced personally that central government are the right people to run specific businesses as their job is to provide and enforce the necessary controls. I do however feel strongly that all the utilities should be owned and run by British companies and British management. We should have the destiny of our own future in our own hands. Having to import coal, gas, and electricity creates a sovereign risk and could breech our security. This might sound dramatic but in truth all major organisations and governments have an innate desire to own, in quotes, the world, and this creates a warring attitude. I would prefer we were in charge of our own destiny.

CHAPTER FIVE

BUDGETS

THE CHANCELLOR'S SHOWPIECE

As with most of my observations I personally relate to the post war years, so information prior to that time is limited but where I think I have some input I will use it.

Nominally every year there is a budget and Parliament debate and pass a Finance Act. This was traditionally in March of each year prior to the end of the Financial Year-end on April 5th. From my memory this always included altering various taxes, both personal and business and should have been an attempt by the Chancellor of the Exchequer to balance the Country's books. The normal period of a Parliament was five years and the budgets would always reflect where we were in the session. A newly elected party with a reasonable majority would to some degree take advantage and get through difficult parts of their program in the first few years. This allowed them to find give-aways just prior to the next election in order to improve their rating with the electorate and hopefully win a further term in office.

Other than the regular updates to personal tax allowances and adjustments to business there was usually some reference to fuel and tobacco levies and wine and spirit taxes. I remember particular announcements that had an impact on life and wellbeing in general. I will try and describe some of these and the resultant outcomes:

The budget is made up and presented as give some take some away scenario and then presented skilfully to hopefully reflect a generous Chancellor. I will now present the two sides of the balancing process.

What is given away and what is taken away are now going to be listed under Government Income and Expenses.

EXPENSES

FAMILY ALLOWANCE was originally an attempt to aid families to bring up more than one child and I think was given in cash weekly to the mother for the second and third child up to a certain age. The rules changed several times over the years usually for one of the aforementioned reasons. This allowance was changed many times and I believe it had periods where all children were included and some when it did not exist. It has been reinvented and later subsumed into other **Child Credits**

OVER 70 PARENT ALLOWANCE was given to one of their children in the form of a tax code enhancement of £75, I remember this would then vary in value based on the then current basic tax rate. When I was receiving it the basic tax rate was often about 30 per cent which meant I saved around £25-28 in a year. It enabled me to contribute to help with my mother's bills. As in many cases she was a widow; living alone on governments benefits.

HOUSING BENEFIT was meant to be a vote winner with the very noble intention of protecting the poorer classes from the then excessive high rental costs in the private sector. Rackmanism!! I believe the parameters for this benefit have changed and that it can now be claimed based on social conditions as well as straight monetary considerations, particularly if **other** benefits are already being claimed.

MIRAS (Mortgage interest relief at source) this was introduced from 1983 in a bid to encourage home ownership; it allowed borrowers tax relief for interest payments on their mortgage. In the budget Geoffrey Lamont raised the tax allowance from £25,000 to £30,000. Unmarried couples with joint mortgages could pool their allowances to £60,000, a provision known as Multiple Mortgage Tax Relief (MMTR). This remained in place until 1988 when Nigel Lawson ended the option to pool from August 1988. He later expressed regret at not having implemented the change to take effect at the time of the budget, as it is generally accepted that the rush to beat the deadline fuelled a sharp increase in house prices.

I recall that this introduction of MIRAS had one of those unintentional outcomes as the lenders, mainly the building societies, decided that if the tax could be shared between a couple then they should consider lending jointly on two incomes. Joint mortgages existed but the criteria for providing them was based on similar lending as that granted to a single person while the main end was to provide legal joint responsibility. The new criteria allowed a couple to borrow a larger amount based the joint incomes giving them an ability to buy a more costly property and the possible outcome would be that if one of the joint mortgagees had reason to quit work or even quit the relationship repayments would be unavailable. This did not appear to cause a problem because in most of the situations the property was sold at that time and the increased value covered repayment of the whole mortgage. After the abandonment of MMTR the value of property stopped its eternal climb and flattened. By this time based on the apparent success of MMTR the Building Societies had started to lend to buy-to-let landlords based more on house values than traditional criteria. In order to get more funds to lend more money the Societies sold their portfolios on to the market place and because of the history sold them at face value. Mistake! The property market fell and a financial crisis followed with at least one key lender going broke and the market being left a massive shortage causing Lehman Bros to go broke. I know this sounds extreme but the Americans got involved in the trading of these packets of private mortgage funds. I also believe the banks should have been aware of this potential as a somewhat similar event had occurred in Canada some years earlier which was managed within the global banking system.

MARRIAGE ALLOWANCE was again a relatively small amount but, I guess, it was actually intended to promote the idea of marriage and to some extent enable the wife to give up work and start a family. I personally liked this but then after our first child my wife never returned to work but stayed home to bring up our ever extending family. Life changed and this allowance was removed from benefits except people born before about 1936. I lost mine. Big brother kept his.

T/V LICENCE was introduced in June 1946 and cost £2 which I equate to about four and a half dog licences and would be about £90 in to-days money. In 2000 the then Labour Government introduced free licences for the over 75 year olds and made it half price for visually disabled. To-day it costs over £150 and they are talking about stopping the free licences to all over 75's not on specific benefits. The collection of this funding has now been passed to the BBC and there are many people who believe that as this was introduced for, at that time, only BBC and ITV and radio it is now not appropriate. To-day it has been morphed into a television/radio receiving charge and therefore should not be needed for pay T/V and that people who use modern technical equipment should not be burdened. Will this be used in the next election campaign and will each side use positively for themselves or negatively against the opposition.

ROAD TAX was an evolution from Vehicle Tax which started at virtually the same time as motor travel became viable. It first appeared in 1888 but was introduced in 1896 for 'light locomotives'. Under the Motor Car Act 1903 all road vehicles were taxed annually at a rate of 20 shillings per year, with the system being administered by county councils. A duty of 20 shillings per horsepower was set in place in 1920 when excise duty was introduced specifically for motor vehicles. In 1921 Tax discs were introduced. This new tax was initially used for building and maintaining roads. As it was paid directly into the 'road fund' it was known as the Road Fund

Licence or road tax. This set the duty at £1 per horsepower. In 1936 road works were being paid for by government grants. The UK Fund was abolished in 1937 and the hypothecation of vehicles came to an end. Most motorists do not realise or understand this and still think they are paying for the upkeep of the roads when they are deemed now to be paying a tax on damage they do to the roads and environment. Mute difference?? There is still no doubt that the roads are out-of-date and in disrepair whoever is responsible. It is almost certain that from this time on it will be a subject in most budgets. More recently the whole world has started to try and save the planet and control the climate. This has crept into all areas as there are numerous lobbyists and entrepreneurs getting in on the act. Needless to say the vehicle taxes are now based on carbon emissions etc. and modern taxes are based on how these affect the environment.

FUEL TAX or petrol duty as it is known was introduced in 1909 at 3d per gallon (circa 4.5 litres). It had doubled to 6d by 1915. It was abolished in 1919 then reintroduced in 1928 at 4d per gallon. From then on it has yo-yoed with annual adjustments and the changes coming into effect on the day of the budget. This used to cause long queues at the petrol pumps immediately after the announcement and prior to the time, later that day, when the change would come into effect. Many people used to wait with their engines running just to put only a few litres in to top-up. In 1993 a 'fuel escalator' was introduced by Chancellor Norman Lamont, This was to start at 10% and then rise annually at 3% above inflation. In 1990 a litre of petrol cost 41p – by 1995 it had risen to 59p and the escalator was raised to 5%.

CHRISTMAS BONUS (U.K.). This £10 bonus to pensioners was first made in1972 and repeated by the Heath Government in 1973 and 1974. It was repeated by the Labour Party in 1977 and 1978. It was established as a permanent fixture in 1979. The payment has remained at £10 only, to this day. This must have been a vote teaser and although the amount now minimal no government would risk upsetting all the old folk by simply abandoning it.

THE WINTER FUEL ALLOWANCE. Introduced by Gordon Brown in 1997 to help pay heating bills. It is a tax free allowance of between £100 and £300 and can apply if you were born before 5th May 1953.The payment is not means tested and paid each year around the beginning of December to any eligible person living between 19-25 September that year. Curiously ex-patriots even if they reside in a hot climate are still able to register and obtain these monies. I am sure this will be a discussion point before and during future election campaigns.

NATIONAL PENSIONS were reviewed annually but more recently particularly as interest rates dropped, it was necessary to alter the system in order for them to keep up with inflation. This was done in stages but culminated in what was described as the 'triple lock'. This committed the Government to raise pensions annually by the highest of three percentages: 2.5%, average earnings or Inflation. As pensions are still reviewed annually this will almost certainly reflect in future budgets as the economy is always in a state of flux and the pension can be seen to be too high or too low giving the

Chancellor a chance to put a positive spin on any announcement.

The following are examples that appear to be sold as benefits in the budget speech as they help the voters but do not directly impact the Government costs. The actual costs finish up being taken by a council or a business. This means the real cost finishes up in your council tax or a rise in living expenses through the resultant inflation.

HOLIDAY ENTITLEMENT. In the early part of the century it was not uncommon for people to work at least a 12 hour day without any paid holiday. This improved when the unions developed and started to negotiate with managers. It became fairly standard for all workers to be given a two week paid holiday but some had restrictions. The factories in the north of England closed for two weeks and told their staff that those two weeks were their annual leave. This became known as a 'workers fortnight' or some variance such as 'wakes or factory'. Real paid holidays came pretty well widespread from the1950's. Since then holidays on the continent, particularly in Germany were commonly at least 21days. Our Government got in on the act and legislated the minimum number of day's holiday a reasonable size company must provide. This was supported with the possibility of fines for not fulfilling the law. The outcome of course was for the staff to feel that the budget had helped them but at the same time their bosses faced the impact of the extra costs. Staff are not officially allowed to take pay in lieu of vacation.

PERKS FOR TEMPORARY STAFF. Around 1970 the benefits that full time staff were receiving became a hot subject and here again new legislation was brought in to equalise a number of these 'quote' perks. And the dictum came out that temps should have equal holiday rights and to be allowed time off for things like doctor and hospital appointments, dentists children's needs etc. Another example where the government dictate but business pays.

YOUTH TRAINING SCHEME (YTS). In this scheme it is not who takes the cost that interested me but rather the rule of unintended consequences. When this was introduced around 1984 it appeared to be a great idea to promote the equivalent of an abbreviated apprenticeship. The idea was that a 16 year old could obtain a job in any part of the community and be paid £50 per week. The employer was of course getting cheap labour but had to provide training and also allow the child to have time off to attend training courses in the business they were pursuing. This was usually on one day and one evening per week and at the end of the two years they would hopefully have obtained and NVQ (National Vocational Qualification). The intended aim was that with this training and the investment that had been made in the individuals they would be offered a full time job on full pay scales. The real outcome was in many circumstances the employer had found that he was gaining significantly from the cheap labour and would at the end of the 2 years lay the person off and start again with a new school leaver.

SALE OF COUNCIL HOUSES was to me a surprise. The idea was that the local councils would sell houses to sitting tenants at a significant discount to the market value. Again this is a Government dictum that had to be managed by the local councils. In this case I do not see the benefits except for the apparent poorer part of society being given a chance to get onto the property ladder. The view from my aspect was to see local councils being unable to house as many of their community on the subsidised rents. I knew a lot of young and not so young people who had been on the waiting list to be housed for more than a decade. I also understood that having sold the council houses they were not allowed by edict to use that money to build more houses. This would not have helped inner city councils anyway as there was no land available for them to buy. As one senior M P said at the time it was tantamount to selling the family silver. However I am sure many people who took up the offer were very happy but I feel that supporting the part of the community that were unable to take advantage or maybe would have been able to live in a council house would have been a better option but could have cost a lot of time and money and would probably have put up the cost of the Council Tax.

MINIMUM WAGE. This is a very social approach but as initially having been set at close to the wage a lot of low earners were getting it was only a hardship to companies that were not treating their staff well enough. As with most good ideas they get do-gooders on the band wagon and then the formula for increasing this minimum on a regular basis becomes the norm and then lots of companies depending on low cost and temporary staff find they are struggling to pay their way. This particularly started to impact the Hospitality sector. As the basic costs were rising companies looked for ways to spread their costs and appeared to create a new type of employment which became known as 'Zero Hour contracts'. In certain businesses this was clearly a way to manage staff and cut costs and get round certain elements of the law regarding things like, holiday entitlement, insurance stamps, redundancy payments etc. There was another side to this coin which said that the agreement suited many people who wanted to be able to run their lives around personal commitments. This meant that as they also had a say in whether they were themselves available for work they could also either look after their children as and when necessary or work in the university holiday. These people could sign up for several different 'zero hour' contracts and cherry pick. This will definitely not go away as either a vote winner or an attack on the opposition.

NATIONAL INSURANCE in this instance I feel I should not explain it here as an expense, as it is really on the other side of the balance sheet. What I want to address is that this was always seen as a stamp and made the payer eligible for health and pension benefits. It was a relatively small sum of money but was down for review in budgets. I feel that this payment has been taken out of context and has to all intents and purposes become income tax and now is charged at around 12% of income and rising.

INCOME

INCOME TAX was first implemented in Great Britain in December 1798 to pay for weapons and equipment for the Napoleonic Wars and was even then graduated based on income. Taxes were collected from 1799-1802 and then abolished but were reintroduced in 1803 and again abolished in 1816 for one year after the Battle of Waterloo. The tax was applied for a 'contribution of the profits arising from property, professions, trades and offices (the words income tax) were deliberately avoided. At this time it was also decreed that tax could be deducted at source and schedules were introduced. These schedules remained pretty unchanged until the Thatcher Government in 1979. However, from this time (circa 1817) onwards the various Governments agreed and disagreed over the need to abolish income tax. The 'Times' in 1874 election coverage said 'It is now evident that whoever is Chancellor when the budget is produced, the income tax will be abolished'. As with many other manifesto promises this did not happen and income tax has stayed with us. Until 1965 companies in some circumstances could pay income tax but at that time corporation tax was introduced. These changes were consolidated by the Income and Corporation Taxes Act 1970. During the First World War there were no sales tax or value added tax. The main increase in revenue came from the income tax, which in 1915, went up to 3/6d, about 17 and 1/2 per cent. The rate grew to 25% in 1915. The highest rate of ,tax peaked in the Second World War at 99.25%, it was then slightly reduced and was around 90% in the 1950s and 60s. In 1971 the top rate of income tax on earned income was cut to 75%. It raised again in1974 to 83%.

Margaret Thatcher favoured indirect taxation and in the first of her Government budgets in 1979 the top rate was reduced from 83% to 60% and the basic rate from 33% to 30%. The rates were reduced steadily until 1988 when the basic rate was 25% and top rate 40%. By 1997 it was down to 23%.

This, of course, does not tell the full story as during this time the National Insurance stamp had been converted from a relatively small weekly or monthly payment into a virtually full blown tax. This is now taken at source at around 12% of the pay packet before deductions. Also where company perks were not included in Income for tax purposes, through a gradual dripping process many perks are now included as salary on the schedule D. These include bonuses paid in dividends, company cars and related expenses and I believe a number of other quote, 'perks' including subsidised company loans and mortgages. I also know that many employees can claim tax deductions for necessary expenses such as clothing and tools, but in the big picture this is relatively small beer.

Income tax will always be a thorn in everyone's side but as evidenced it is here to stay and will be a vote winner or loser in many future elections. There are endless opportunities for the Governments to change the scaled amounts of tax relief and to include or exclude various classes of society. This could be by varying different groups for different levels of relief or simply changing the criteria for inclusion or exclusion of more or fewer exceptions to the need to pay tax. Pensioners and the self-employed are open targets, or maybe help the disabled and long term sick.

CUSTOMS DUTIES and this includes excise duties. Right from before income tax the Governments and/or the realm exacted import and export duties from businessmen. These taxes were about after the second war and even after the excise had taken their bit the Government got the banks to collect a further stamp duty on all of the bills of exchange used to pay for imports and exports.

STAMP DUTY was another aspect and this was introduced in 1853. Before I go on I would like to explain at this point this type of announcement was not always included in the Chancellors speech but only in the full text passed to be debated in the passing of the Finance Act later. In this way, right up to this day, we listen to the speech and often misinterpret or are led by the nose on the things the Chancellor would like us to concentrate on. In truth there have been many instances over the years where the general public seemed unaware of the full effect until it was already in law. As an aside I have what to me is a strong memory of misinterpretation; the press did not listen to the precise words when the Chancellor, Gordon Brown, announced that all pensioners would receive a minimum of £150 a week. The red top papers led the next day on pensions are to go up to a minimum of £150. In truth pensions did not change but anyone receiving less than £150 were guaranteed some form of benefit to fill the gap. Back to stamp duty until 1853 cheques were illegal if dated or negotiated more than 10 miles from the bank on which they were drawn but this act legalised such cheques if they bore an impressed or adhesive penny postage stamp. The distance restriction was removed in 1858 and in 1881 an adhesive stamp inscribed 'postage & revenue' could be used. In 1918 stamp duty was doubled to 2d and by 1929 the Exchequer was coining about 3.5 million pounds per year. In 1956 the banks were allowed to issue chequebooks with stamp duty already in place. This duty was abolished in 1971 just before decimalisation and entry to the common market. I am sure some new form of tax was either introduced or other taxes were amended to make up the shortfall. Another stamp duty is that applied on the purchase of houses and this has seen many crude changes and given home buyers headaches.

PURCHASE TAX. Between 1940 and 1973 the UK had a consumption tax called purchase tax, which was levied at different rates depending on goods' luxuriousness. This was applied to the wholesale price at a rate of 33 1/3%. This was doubled in April 1942 to 66 2/3%, and further increased in April 1943 to a rate of 100% before reverting in April 1946 to 33 1/3% again. Unlike VAT, purchase tax was applied at the point of manufacture and distribution, not at the point of sale. The rate of purchase tax at the start of 1973, when it gave way to VAT, was 25%. On January 1st 1973 the UK joined the European Economic Community and as a consequence purchase tax was replaced by Value Added Tax (VAT), on 1st April 1973. The Conservative Chancellor Lord Barber set a single VAT rate (10%) on most goods and services. VAT has remained since and there was pressure for the UK to maintain parity with the Europeans but we did retain some of our exemptions and varied rates. The rate has altered over the years, but for many years on most items has been 20%. Exceptions include zero on children's clothes and some other items while the tax on domestic fuel is only 12 ½%. This kind of tax has always given the Chancellor an opportunity to impact inflation.

CAPITAL GAINS TAX was pre-empted by a short term gains tax beginning in1962, which was aimed exclusively at speculative gains. Gains made on shares and securities held for less than three months – and those made on land held for less than three years – were taxed as income.

Capital Gains Tax was first introduced in 1965 on gains made on the disposal of assets by individuals, personal representatives and trustees. It comprised short term gains tax – by which taxable assets acquired and realised within twelve months were assessed to income tax – and, a long term tax on assets held over one year, which were charged at 30%. The tax applied to the total net gains realised in a tax year on assets, save those specifically exempted. Since 1971 there has been only one comprehensive tax on capital gains.

Prior to 2008, capital gains were treated as the top slice of income, and the tax was charged at the same rates as savings income. In October the chancellor announced a major reform of CGT: the withdrawal of taper relief and indexation relief, and the introduction of a single rate tax from April 2008.This was and is a complicated tax and gives government endless opportunities for future variations and tweaks that they may feel might help balance their budget. As mentioned before these are the kind of changes that do not hit the headlines but can significantly impact the electorate on the end of them.

INHERITANCE TAX is a tax on the estate (the property, money and possessions) of someone who's died. There is normally no inheritance tax to pay if the value of your estate is below £325,000 or you leave everything over £325000 to your spouse, civil partner, a charity or a community sports club. If you are married or in a civil partnership and your estate is worth less than your threshold, any unused threshold can be added to your partner's threshold when you die. Standard rate of tax is 40% but only on the amount above the threshold. If you leave more than 10% of your total assets to charity the rate can be reduced to 36%. There are reliefs and exemptions for things like lifetime gifts and business relief where certain assets can be passed on free of tax.

There are a number of ways lawyers and accountants try to get round some of the rules by drawing up trusts etc. but the government become aware of these and have been known to close the loophole retrospectively.

There is a widespread belief that this tax apart from being a very unfair tax and sometimes difficult and expensive to execute, it is also double taxation as usually assets are bought from taxed income. The poor look at this as reasonable as it taxes the richest whereas the rich see it, as it were, as a last nail in the coffin by the nasty anti-establishment Tax Collectors. Another area where the Chancellor rubs his hands together at the thought of having another string to his bow.

POLL TAX. It is not always the public that are not given the full picture or something gets missed in translation. The poll tax was going to be a 'coup d'état' for Margaret Thatcher, but, it is my belief, that she understood that as everyone was bound by law to register to vote there was a single comprehensive data base of everybody in the U K . This may or may not have been true but the local councils and their unions appeared to get together and decide that each council would have to create its own local independent data base specifically for this tax. Dare I say from then on chaos reigned?

The aim of her poll tax was that it should be paid by the individual and not based on property rateable values and would therefore be more equitable. When it was introduced my children seemed in general to approve and thought it only right that their father paid less and they contributed. This was not how the press and public in general saw it and it was basically the downfall of Mrs Thatcher. I am not sure that what came next was really any improvement but the local councils got control of this and a new COUNCIL TAX was created. This still exists and each year based on a scaled rating for each premises a levy is raised. This is in part funded by Government grants which can rise and fall and come and go virtually at any time. Central Government will limit by a percentage the maximum amount by which a local council may raise the tax year on year but this does not also apply to other bodies such as County Councils and police forces which the local councils have no control over but have to simply include these in the overall billing. If the problem with the poll tax was partly to do with the ability to collect the funds the new system seems to have failed miserably when you see the massive sums that remain unpaid each year. Having said this I would not like another upheaval for some time to come and trust that when it happens it has been properly thought out. Maybe allow some Ministry to have full responsibility to manage the local calculations and ensure the money is used for the intended purposes.

BUSINESS RATES or non-domestic rates, are a tax on the occupation of non-domestic property (NNDR). These Rates are a property tax with ancient roots that was formerly used to fund local services that was formalised with the Poor

Law 1582 and superseded by the Poor Law of 1601. The local Government Finance Act 1988 introduced business rates from 1990, repealing its immediate predecessor, the General Rate Act 1967. The Local Government Finance Act 1988, with follow up legislation, provided a fresh administrative framework for assessing and billing but did not redefine the legal unit of property, the hereditament that had been developed through rating case law.

Business Taxes have never been a popular tax and have been administered both, at different times, by Local councils and Government. Needless to say these always conflict as all the nation is not equal and therefore local business and for similar reasons local councils felt as though they also suffered. Within the business community it also felt that applying the same criteria to shops, factories and industrial estates was disproportionate to the actual costs of running these premises. Local Authorities have also been keen to regain full control over business rates as they often accuse the government of underfunding them through central grants that impose additional duties that they must also fulfil. This is the third largest expense to most businesses after rent and wages. There have been many adjustments to how these are managed and since The Valuation Office Agency, an executive agency of HM Revenue & Customs, has had a statutory duty to prepare local ratings every five years containing rateable values for all non-domestic properties, disagreements have never gone away. When these ratings have been set a multiplier known as the Uniform Business Rate (UBR) is then used by the local authority to calculate what percentage of the rateable value of the property has to be paid in business rates. The multiplier is set annually by the Government. This is definitely not a natural vote catcher but because of regional differences can and has been used to change the perceived help the Government is giving to hopefully Impact voting in different parts of the country.

COST OF MEDICAL PRESCRIPTIONS. When the National Health Services was established in 1948 all prescriptions were free. The power to make as charge was introduced in the NHS Amendment Act 1949, and proposals for charges were a factor in the resignation of Aneurin Bevan from the Labour Government in 1951. Charges were introduced in 1952, by the Conservative Party, at a rate of 1 shilling per prescription. In 1956 the rules were changed so that a charge applied to each item prescribed. In 1961 it was doubled to 2s. Charges were abolished by the Wilson government on 1st February 1965, but re-introduced on 10th June 1968 at the higher rate of 2s 6d, but with a wider range of exemptions. These charges have been increased regularly with annual increases becoming the norm.

In the early days of prescriptions it was left to the person submitting to complete the back of the form in order to make clear that they either had to pay the standard rate or that they were exempted. It would appear that many people abused the system and claimed exemption and did not appear to be identified and/or prosecuted. In this regard there was a time when I asked, in all innocence, of a young neighbour what the current rate for a prescription was. To my surprise she did not know and simply told me it cost nothing as you just had to sign the back. It turned out that her parent's had always handled the process until she had her first child when as an exempt person she was entitled to complete the back of the form. She then never realised that a year later she should have been paying for her personal prescriptions. Do not think she was alone in this approach. Many years later, possibly into the 2000's, the Government decided that it appeared to them that doctors were giving too many pills out, particularly to the elderly. This was based on one of these 'quote' dubious surveys that said when people died a mountain of pills were taken way in the local rubbish. At that time it was standard for doctors to prescribe two months of medication which was then reduced to just 30 days. Here again I see the government being influenced by lobbyist groups or had what they felt were good intentions. The result which has not to my knowledge been tested was that administration at least doubled in the doctors surgeries as this appears to have the obvious outcome of doubling the number of prescriptions being issued and, on the back of this, doubling the work of the pharmacies. The extra paper must also contribute and patients in many cases chose to go to the doctor each time they needed a review; thereby creating more appointments. This is an area where, as I mentioned earlier, the old fashioned Civil Servants would have done some analysis and advised their relative minister of these possible events, but, as I also said earlier, people's responsibilities in the organisation seem to have changed and there is no longer a proper team or management functioning effectively. I will address the ability or not of the NHS to help solve this type of problem under a wider discussion later. I must also say here that an evident outcome of doubling the number of prescriptions would surely statistically have doubled the Government income and helped the Chancellor balance the books.

UNIVERSITY FEES. This is slightly out of the years that I intended to cover as it extends into the 2000's but I do have an opinion that I would like to express and particular with regard to exorbitant fees that were introduced in 1998 just after Tony Blair became prime minster. I will get to this later but now to some history.

There have been seismic changes in the scale and structure over the last 100 years and student experience has changed dramatically. Prior to the Second World War the general perception in political circles was based on the Oxford and Cambridge scenario but there were in fact many provincial universities such as Leeds and Nottingham. These took in predominantly local students who travelled on local transport to college each day. The majority of the 60% who were locally educated were brought up by and living with families that had never moved more than a few miles in their entire lives. One outcome of this was explained to me in the early fifties with regard to Sheffield by a graduate from that university. We were working in London and he said that many of his fellow graduates had opted to take jobs working on the factory floors of the major cutlery companies rather than move away. These students had been funded through to their degree on state scholarships which were highly prized and few and far between or through a patchy system of local authority provision, but there was also a lot of small bursaries awarded by schools, universities and charitable bodies. The lions' share of support actually came in the form of grants from the Board of Education, made in return for a 'pledge' or commitment to teaching as a career following graduation. The grant could be reclaimed if this did not happen.

After 1945 the system remained pretty well the same and when I left school in 1954 it had been suggested to me that I stay on for 'A' levels with the intention of applying for a university place. I actually just wanted to go out to work and follow a career. I was unable to become an apprentice in architecture as the grammar school had not taught technical drawing which was a pre-requisite. I started on a graduated pay system in a British bank and actually earnt little more than I would have been able to obtain in grants. In 1960 the Ministry of Education referred the question of grants to the Anderson Committee. This recommended a national system whereby every student enrolling on a degree course for the first time became eligible for a grant towards tuition fees and maintenance. This level to be based on student income. This meant that young people could now choose to go to universities away from home. This golden age did not last longs inflation chipped away at the real value of maintenance allowances, but students still got their tuition fees paid- these escaped parental means test applicable to maintenance.

A darker age set in with the introduction of student loans in1990. Maintenance grants were first frozen and then reduced annually until 1998. From 1998 students were required to pay a standard contribution to the cost of their tuition fees. These costs could be funded by a Government sponsored loan, managed by a subsidiary of a government agency. This became a prime topic of the political agenda. I think we are now back to where I started as Tony Blair came to power one year before these changes in 1997.

I have always felt, and still do, that education should have the same aims as the NHS and be ostensibly free. Making students rack up a loan prior getting a proper job is to me unacceptable. This of course has to some degree been recognised, and the loans do not have to commence a repayment schedule until the graduate obtains a certain level of income set at about the amount of average income.

In practice the system was another of those bright ideas that looked good when presented on paper but appears to have failed miserably in practice because I understand that a significant number of the loans will not be repaid in the lifetime of the graduate and in a lot of cases the graduate will not even earn enough money to start repaying the loan. In the meantime with the drive to encourage more students to attend university we have seen a much higher percentage dropping out and not completing the degree course. Others will discontinue working and stop repayment. Current figures indicate that the loan debt has soared into the billions and that this means that a proper funding system with, maybe, slightly fewer graduates would not have overall cost the taxpayer a significantly different amount. This will later be put more into context when I address education and goals for university entrants, the conversion of technical colleges to universities and moving the school leaving age to 18.

FINES. When I was a kid I thought that the only people who could fine a member of the public was the Courts. I still think that this was true. In those days drunks and prostitutes were arrested in the late evening and taken before the 'beak' at 10 o'clock the next morning. At this time George Orwell wrote 1984 and we all thought he was "out of this world" but the future soon changed and now often feels like Big Brother has arrived. The comedian/singer Max Bygraves, sang about 'Thing's ain't what they use to be' and telling us that they had put parking meters outside our doors to greet us. This is my earliest recollection of a body (Local Council) outside the courts being enabled to collect penalty fines.

The police now have many fixed penalty fines which are either administered on the spot or advised and taken to headquarters for assessment. Speeding for instance can be a fine and penalty points on your licence or an offer to attend an awareness course. The fine and the awareness course cost similar amounts but if you are offered and take up on the course you will avoid the penalty points. We are told that the police only cover administration fees but you do feel they do in real terms administer for a small profit. In no special order the list below gives the offences that come to mind.

Parking. These are also handled directly by councils.

Obstruction.

Speeding.

Using Mobile Phones in vehicles.

Seat belt violations. (This started as driver only and has progressed to, front seat and then all passengers some making the driver responsible and others that made the passenger take the can.

Child Seats operated similar to seat belts.

Smoking. First in cars (with young children in them) and later private businesses and public places.

Litter in public spaces which can also be council led.

There are multiple awareness courses and these can be an offer in a lot situations.

To Joe Public most of these innovations are seen as 'cash cows' and keep the more important job of regular policing undermanned. As it is impossible to be totally equitable and ensure that all transgressions are addressed people are sometimes heard to wonder if when they are caught the copper was just looking for an excuse to get back to the nick for a bit of warmth and a cup of coffee.

These fines are somewhat arbitrary but they are being managed by known and accepted public bodies i.e. the police and local councils. A much more worrying kind of fine is now being handed out by unelected QUANGO'S. As mentioned in the introductory passages many of these government sponsored groups are related to the utility companies or identified sectors of the business world. A short, but not comprehensive list of these would include water, gas/electricity, telecoms in the utilities and banking, insurance, auditing, retail, company boards and oil. I am at this point not looking at the amount of power they have over management practices but the fact that they can actually fine groups either as a body or address a particular perceived transgression by one of their members. I could really get on my high horse but will limit my remarks to a couple of examples to give a feel of the problem. I stress that this is a personal view but most of these quangos would appear to be run by ex-senior members of the specific environment/industry they were employed in, who have taken an opportunity to move on, at a time when they were steadily getting out of touch with the speed of change and innovation. Here my quote is that those that can, DO, and those that cannot TEACH. In this case teaching is more loosely translated in audit/criticise and/or worse become little dictators. Take water for example when these people were in charge there was little or no work done on the necessary replacements needed to the old and rusting mains but they saw it in their remit to fine one of the southern water boards millions of pounds over for what appeared to be a long term maintenance problem. To add to my worry was the fact there was no evidence that this money was to be reinvested to, perhaps, address the shortcoming. My natural reaction was that money had been taken from a company that needed to invest in the future and that the only way they could satisfy this problem was to pour money into it and, as an outcome, increase the cost to the end user (the householder). This kind of thing has been repeated frequently and there is nobody checking whether these criticisms were justified or even that they were beneficial, for instance, could technology have been in the pipeline to give a much better outcome. We cannot vote these people out but I thought that in one of the Teresa May manifestos she promised to shut down all the quangos. At that time I said, power to her elbow, but modern politics prevailed and another election promise was overturned. I still think that fines should be reserved for breaking the law and should be handled by the courts.

Creating your own laws and then making up your own fines is not a satisfactory situation.

OTHER INCOME. These do not always provide direct income as the next two actions actually reduced previous years' expenses. First Tax relief on dividends was stopped. This significantly impacted the amount of money institutions, and in particular pension providers earned from investments, suddenly faced the full cost of tax instead of receiving a reasonable % relief. Secondly Tax on pension savings was capped with similar repercussions. Mr Brown introduced both of these in either his first or at least, an early budget and the impact was in essence to wipe out the viability of final salary pension schemes. On its own it was dramatic but at the same time he also changed the way the long term strength of pension funds were audited. Up until this point the funds were checked regularly by actuaries but he now wanted dynamic accounting. Overnight many funds were deemed to have a significant shortfall and boards of directors were forced to transfer monies into their pension funds. This also meant some companies went to the wall and employees lost out on what they expected as a full pension and in some cases were out of work as well. I felt quite strongly that if it is not broke do not try to fix it. This change should have had much better analysis and then if necessary a new method should have been managed into place.

There are a few other incomes that I consider were contrived simply to create a quick income from areas that, in truth, had no alternative but to comply and again it cost the man in the street. I refer to air travel duty, offender levy, rail fares to be raised annually by a specific % above inflation each year and insurance premium tax.

On top of all the budget items that have gone before there are of course several stand-by options for every budget; these are wine, beer, spirits and tobacco. Checking the price increases over the years will evidence how astutely **these** have been modified or perhaps manipulated. Maybe I am a cynic but it is easy to hit a sitting target, in this case pleasure and addiction.

BUDGET SUMMARY COMMENTS.

The preceding opinions have been made with particular reference to the impact they have within the annual budget but many of these subjects are much broader and will be discussed later in their full context as individual topics. I did not make it clear when I introduced quangos how I thought they were actually part of the regular budget but there are also announcements made by the Chancellor that lead the way to future changes and I think he would have introduced the idea of these control bodies in order to get over the point that he was in charge and in fact taking charge. Particularly telling company boards that they must have executive directors, equal representation of the sexes and green policies which supports my opinion that politicians are always aware of the lobbyists and the electorate as portrayed by the press.

CHAPTER SIX

FREEDOM OF INFORMATION ACT

This is my last item relating specifically to Central Government and it does not need a lot from me except to quote Tony Blair who was himself the architect of this piece of law. Some years after he had left parliament he was speaking somewhere when he was encouraged to talk about this act and he said it is probably the thing I regret most out of all the time I was in charge.

This would seem an appropriate point to mention openness which was probably what encouraged the thoughts on the need for a freedom of information act. I feel strongly that demanding openness in every walk of life is totally inappropriate. The trauma of being told the truth can often outweigh the results of keeping quiet. This is particularly true when considering the local doctor. Can he not be sparing with the whole truth for the sake of wellbeing. The end product of this demand for openness seems to have created a reaction that has resulted in, the press particularly, and politicians feeling a need to know what has been decided or what is going to be announced tomorrow. I long for the days when not everything had to be leaked and I can look forward to hearing the budget from the chancellor first at the time of his speech. I still like a good surprise and do not always want to hear the bad news. It should not be compulsory. Maybe we could also re-introduce common sense back into everyday habits.

CHAPTER SEVEN

LOCAL GOVERNMENT

Having just handled National Government it would seem a natural progression to move on to local Government. This also follows the pattern that I intend to use in choosing the progressive subjects throughout the book which will be based on perceived inception date. In the case of local Government this has be around since the year 'dot' with feudalism and local hams and small towns which were basically self- managed. After a short history lesson I will then address how things have progressed from the beginning of the 1900's and will look at Parish councils, district councils, borough councils and county councils.

I have the same feelings about the progression, in the 1900's, for local Government as I have written about central Government in that it moved ostensibly from a vocational task to a business career. That said the local government structure has a good history. Here goes with the history lesson.

Anglo Saxon local 700 – 1066

Norman Conquest 1066 – 1100

Medieval period 1300- 1500

> The decline of the feudal system

> County corporate (an extension of the borough system).

Later changes in local government 1500 – 1832   Parishes

Great Reform Act 1832

Municipal Corporation Act

   Public reforms

   Expansion of the franchise

Local Government Act 1888

Attempts at reform 1945

As you can see there was little change in the early 1900s which was in essence various levels of government from the bottom up or the top down, whichever way you look at it. Start at the bottom and you go from the smallest to the largest and their scope is relative to this size. All levels are voted in by their electorate and have responsibility directly to them, but if you look from the top down you will find that as in most lines of business the top level pass down directives and restrict certain actions. The local government function that everybody think they understand is what they look at as the local council. This is the borough or town council and they administer all local budgetary needs. They do not however actually make all the key decisions particularly with regard to highways, rate collection, business rates transport and fixed rate fines etc. That said they do prepare an annual budget and advise all the households and businesses how they have reached the rates they are going to collect over the following twelve months.

Here I will now tell you not the official process but how I see it. Key dates are from 1945 – 1972. All the governments in that period tried desperately to make significant reform but either could not decide what action to take, or were thwarted by central or local activists or the unions. It was also in this period that the volunteer vocational councillor became the semi-professional. I do not think I can say that from getting only nominal expenses for attending meetings they became paid ancillaries but it did seem to the man in the street that a significant ground change had taken place. The thing we did not see was that the new breed had not actually changed their colours in that they were still amateur management. I say this because of the actions where I lived in the 1990s. The local council announced that as the previous party in power had failed to properly manage the parking in the district (especially the multi-storey car parks) they had decided to give a contract to NCP who would guarantee them a profit and improve the lighting and access facilities. This was to be with no price increases. True in the short term but we were not told this was only a 5 year deal and, guess what, after 5 years costs rose dramatically. They also appeared to not fully support the local retailers and gave significant planning permission to small Tesco stores. I was obviously not the only person that saw this a mistake when some bright spark added to the welcome to the town signage a caption reading, sponsored by NCP & Tesco. I never felt that the local treasury department fully understood what the word budget really meant and this appeared to be confirmed when I met a retired manager from that department. I questioned what he felt a budget was, his reply was it what you spend. When I told him that if my household budget was run on that basis I would always overspend. He replied that the council was different and that they had a duty to fulfil many commitments and if they caused an over spend, so be it. Asked how he would account for this and to whom he simply advised me that they would increase the taxes the following year to cover the costs. I did have some sympathy when he evidenced the various projects that were foisted on the department after the tax had been set. These included reductions in government grants, taking over elements of road maintenance from the Highways etc.

Despite what I have just said or, implied I do think that there are a lot of very dedicated councillors trying to do a very necessary job to the best of their ability. I am still reminded, though, of the picture I saw of a fisherman with his trousers around his ankles and still struggling to bring in his catch. Presumably his efforts had parted his lower clothing from his upper body. This had not appeared significant in the circumstances. People go into local politics with a specific passion they would like to action. They often get assigned to a further passion on various committees. I feel they get so absorbed in their involvement and often over commitment that they forget to 'pull their trousers up' and get on with the real job in hand which is managing the local economy. They, in other words gradually lose touch with the real world and forget what they were elected to do. This happens in all walks of life and particularly in the professions such as teaching, banking, finance, and insurance where the areas are a closed shop and tradition remains stronger than the recognition for change based on the outside changes to the environment.

CHAPTER EIGHT

POST OFFICE

ALL ASPECTS

Here again I will start with a potted history and then follow it with my memories and comments.

Post Office branches, along with the Royal Mail delivery service, were formerly part of the General Post Office and after 1969, the Post Office Corporation. Post Office Counters Ltd was created as a wholly owned subsidiary of the Post Office Corporation in 1986. Prior to this The Royal or the British postal service started life around 1516.

1516 Henry VII established a 'Master of Posts', a position which evolved into the office of the Postmaster General.

1635 Charles 1 made the postal service available to the public with postage being paid by the recipient.

1654 Oliver Cromwell granted a monopoly over mail delivery service in England to the 'Office of Postage'.

1657 Fixed postal rates were introduced.

1660 Charles II established the General Post Office.

1661 The Postage date stamp was first used, and the first Postmaster General was appointed.

1784 The first mail coach was introduced

1793 Uniformed post men hit the streets for the first time.

1830 First mail train from Liverpool to Manchester made it first deliveries

1837 Rowland Hill, a schoolmaster from Birmingham, invented the adhesive postage stamp for which he was knighted.

1838 The Post Office money order system was introduced.

1840 The first adhesive stamp, the Penny Black, was released nationally, and the Uniform Penny Post, by which letters could be sent for one penny, was established.

1852 The Post Office pillar box was erected in Jersey.

1853 First post boxes were erected on the mainland.

1857 the first wall boxes were installed.

1870 The Post Office launched its telegraph service. Postcards were issued and a fixed rate of 1/2d applied. Newspaper wrappers were introduced.

1880 Postmen began to use bicycles.

1881 The Postal order was introduced

1883 Parcel post began.

1912 The Post Office opened its national telephone service.

To all intents and purposes the system remained relatively unchanged until 1968 when second class stamps were introduced and National Giro Bank opened.

 At this stage the post office was part of everyday life in all villages and towns across England and were a government agency for services such as over the counter cashing of benefit giros issuing T/V licences, handling driving licence applications and renewing car tax discs. They were an intermediary for passport applications and some other government interfaces. In 1969 the General Post Office changed from a Government department to a Nationalised Industry and in 1979 had their first strike over pay. From this time on several good and bad changes came into effect. The postcodes were introduced right across Britain, the telegram was abolished and the remainder of the business split into three and renamed the Post Office Group and two years later the Postal workers held another strike 17 years after the first one.

In the background the government started to, in many ways, undermine the functions of the Post Office by outsourcing key money earners from the Postmasters. Giro cheques could be paid into ordinary bank accounts, T/V licences bought in Tesco, dog licences were stopped, and regular mail could be handled in bulk for businesses by licenced businesses, as could parcel post. Post Offices started to go out of business. Later when modern banking started to move into electronics and they started to close remote branches, where the old post offices could have stepped in to service the local community it was now ill prepared. I think I am back to lack of forward thinking within government. They had by the way sold the Giro Bank to a building Society by then.

CHAPTER NINE

NATIONAL HEALTH SERVICE

The ideas for a National Health Service can be traced back to the early 1900s with a minority report of the Royal Commission on the Poor Law in 1909. It was argued that a new system was needed to replace the antiquated ideas of the Poor Law which was still in existence from the times of the workhouses in the Victorian era. Although there were good strong arguments this was disregarded by the Liberal Government. Nevertheless more and more people were beginning to speak out and be proactive. Dr Benjamin Moore, a Liverpool physician wrote his ideas down in 'The Dawn of the Health Age' and was probably the first person to use the phrase 'National Health Service' and this led to the creation of the State Medical Association in 1912 but it was another 30years before his ideas would feature in the Beveridge plan for the NHS.

Before the creation of the NHS or anything like it, when someone found themselves needing a doctor or to use medical facilities, patients were generally expected to pay for these treatments. By 1941, the Ministry of health was in the process of agreeing a post-war health policy with the aim that services would be available to the entire general public.

I was a young kid at this time and from memory and hearsay both of my brothers were sent to a fever hospital suffering from scarlet fever. Which I think was funded from a London local borough policy. Soon after their return my twin brother and I both had mumps and measles but were attended by the local doctor for which my mother had to pay around 2/6d per visit. Later my twin also suffered another problem which I know particularly worried the doctor who gave him what was then known as M & B tablets. In this instance he promised to return before his next morning surgery when to our horror the road was covered in snow and it was still snowing. We were more than delighted when the doctor arrived on time in his nice car. The treatment continued and was successful but caused my mother a headache as she had no money except for food money with which to pay her dues. I will always remember hearing the doctor say it would be alright as he could sort it out in due course. After being bombed out in the war we later returned to London and lived round the corner from this same doctor who attended to my mother's needs, albeit we moved some miles away, until he retired having in the meantime extracted my brother and my tonsils in the local hospital along the way. You see our G P was also a local surgeon.

The whole project was brought together after Clement Attlee came to power in 1945 and Aneurin Bevan became Health Minister. The project was based on three ideas expressed in the launch on 5th July 1948. The values were, firstly, that the service helped everyone, healthcare was free and lastly, that care would be provided based on need rather than ability to pay.

In the early years of the NHS expenditure exceeded all expectations and consideration was given to making charges for prescriptions to cover rising costs. The prosperous 1960s saw many adjustments and particularly significant development in availability of drugs.

In about 1974 economical changes were made to reflect the waning economy. In the 1980s, modern methods of management were introduced, but despite having made these changes the NHS remained a critical mainstay service for the British public and was prioritised by Mrs Thatcher despite of other welfare conflicts.

That was the formal history. Now I will talk about my personnel experiences, perceived changes within the structure and management and what I class as an abuse of a public service (taken over by what is often called 'Human Rights').

Let me start with the earlier days when as I and I believe most of the public understood, what the NHS was created for. I thought that the intention was to give free medication to anyone who was ill or injured. This meant that if I had an accident and broke a limb I would be able to be treated at the local hospital, maybe after having called an ambulance. If I had an allergic reaction to a food or medicine I could immediately obtain free help. Examples of this are when I appeared to have broken my arm in two places and was taken by ambulance to the local hospital and when a school friend needed an X-ray after an accident in the playground. On these occasions both the patient and escort were entered into the emergency department for assessment and action. In the absence of telephones in most houses the three hour wait, yes three hours for review, X-ray to be physically processed and then reviewed (well over half hour) and then in the case of a break set in plaster, with no messages home to advise parents what had happened. We were totally appreciative of the service and it was at least as good as we expected. My brother had an accident at work and was given a high dose of penicillin and later in the middle of the night he was in pain and covered in what looked like ulcers. I put him on the pillion of my motor scooter and we were in an out of the emergency department within about an hour and had a positive analysis and appropriate medicine. This is what it is all about. The same efficiency was given to things like appendicitis.

It was not that many years later that new drugs became available and things like contraceptive pills started to be issued on prescription. This did not seem a bad idea but it did not conform to my idea of the NHS to repair and cure. We took our first steps into preventive medicine. This was followed by things like IVF which was to create a fertility that did not exist naturally. I have nothing but good to say about these scientific developments but I felt that they were over and above the aims of the NHS and should have been introduced as a personal service and should have been paid for by the 'quote' the patient. These kinds of provisions by the NHS have to my mind spiralled out of control and the whole area should be reviewed so that the service can be managed within a sensible budget without the encumbrances of ancillary services. You may think that I am uncaring but as a business decision this is simple common sense.

I think I said that in about 1974/ 80s the NHS made significant management changes and since that time whenever money has been poured into the NHS a considerable disproportion has been to either increase the many levels of managers or to give pay increases which also add to their very ample pensions. We do not need more managers we just need more efficiency and better management. When I was in hospital for a hernia operation the ward system was simple and easily understood. At that time you had two levels of qualification for nurses and an ability to gain promotion through further exams or proven ability. The ward had a Matron (Supervisor) and as required senior and junior nurses. These were supported by cleaners and ancillary maintenance and cooking staff and doctors attended daily. Dare I say that it worked? Today you apparently cannot become a nurse without having gained a degree at university, where one usually aspires to a career and promotion. What happened to the adage that nursing was a vocation and that many young aspired to it and learnt the profession through in-house training. This was not dissimilar to traditional apprenticeships. I blame these what I now class as shortcomings onto government and union interference along with the totally over managed environment. This has created a less efficient and more expensive NHS.

A further significant change was made to the General Practice doctoring. I earlier spoke about the dedication of our family doctor who in fact would come to visit day or night in any emergency. When visiting a patient he would take in the perspective of the whole household and in many cases be an earlier identifier of poverty and abuse. This was completely abandoned when doctors were put onto contract with uplifts and incentives. At the time it was not uncommon for a doctor to be earning in excess of 100,000 thousand pounds per annum. By not taking night calls and utilising locums for out of hours they gained a more comfortable life and did not appear to lose out on income. This on its own must have cost the NHS a relative king's ransom but at the same time various clinics were to be created which would benefit the doctor's practice by a fixed sum for each registered patient. These were, I believe, in the first place only main groups like asthmatics and diabetics but is now covering a wider range of groups. Also we think of the flu jab as something the doctors agree everyone should have although many doctors do not participate. Dare I say that the blanket income per jab has probably now increased from the 50 pence it once paid? I understand that there is also a profit to be made from statins. Returning to diabetes with this, as with statins (medication to reduce cholesterol), the diagnosis levels have reduced the margins to such a degree that millions of patients now join the groups that provide the doctors with potential cash per diagnosed patient. This does not feel like an improvement in the service but to some degree an encumbrance as more people have to attend regular follow up checks.

During this time the government in its wisdom deemed that there was a massive wastage of drugs at a high cost to the NHS as they were discarded for various reasons or were unused when people died. They decided that to decrease the wastage they would instruct doctors to prescribe only one month's worth of prescription instead of the then current two. I do not know what the expected savings were estimated at but I cannot believe that it came anywhere near the cost of:

1. The doctor possibly being visited twice as frequently,

2. The extra paperwork involved

3. Doubling the work at the pharmacy.

4. The extra stress on the patient because of shorter deadlines.

It would appear that as a result of two things; the increase of young female doctors who wish to have a family life and the significant increase in potential incomes we now have more doctors doing less hours for more money. It is claimed that the NHS is short of trained doctors. Is this really true?

It is about time we drastically cut the middle management and centralised things like buying and ensured all the hospitals and surgeries were using totally compatible computer systems for a start. X-rays and blood tests should be available almost immediately or certainly the next day.

Again, after all I have said I have never been failed by the NHS and have in fact every reason to thank them, I have no criticism of the work that the front line staff do day in and day out.

CHAPTER TEN

TRADE UNIONS

The Trades Union Congress (TUC) is a national organisation of British trade unions. It is the sole national trade union. Founded in 1868, the TUC held annual conferences of independent unions to promote trade union principles.

The first Congress passed a resolution 'that it is highly desirable that the trades of the United Kingdom should hold an annual congress, for the purpose of bringing trades into closer alliance, and to take action in all Parliamentary matters pertaining to the general interests of the working classes'.

From 1871 it had a permanent standing committee, the Parliamentary Committee, whose principal function was to lobby Parliament for legislation favourable to the unions. The TUC comprised almost exclusively unions of skilled workers until 1889, when it began to accept the first affiliations of 'new' or unskilled general unions. But the TUC's organisation remained extremely rudimentary, and rather than enlarge its own role, it helped to establish two new separate bodies: the General Foundation of Trade Unions, founded in 1899 as an insurance fund for strikes, and the Labour Party. The latter sponsored candidates for Parliament until after 1918, when it became a national political party.

The TUC assumed its modern form after World War I, when it replaced the Parliamentary Committee with a General

Council that could better represent the diverse industrial unions of the British labour movement. The council acquired powers to deal with inter-union conflicts and to intervene in disputes with employers, and it helped mobilise unions during the nationwide General Strike of 1926. In the 30s and 40s, the TUC became the unchallenged representative of industrial labour in dealings with the government, and it participated closely in the management of British industries during World War II.

In the decades that followed that war, the TUC helped shape the economic policy in cooperation with government and business. Its status was secure until 1979, when the Conservative Party came to power under Prime Minister Margaret Thatcher. Excluded from government policy making, the TUC was unable to rally its members against the Thatcher government's legal restrictions on trade unions. These and other factors caused the TUC's membership to decline from about 12 million in 1979 to about 6.6 million at the end of the century.

Unions affiliated with the TUC act autonomously, conducting negotiations independently of the national union. While the TUC is not itself affiliated with any political party, many of its affiliate unions support the Labour Party.

My take on the unions is that in the early part of the 1900s they did a significant amount of good work in lifting the working class people out of the virtual slums and into a proper part of society. I have already mentioned the changes in working conditions and practices that came about prior to the Second World War.

There were however 8 significant strikes between 1891 & 1991

1. 1898 the Welsh Coal which claimed 15 million working days and failed in its aims
2. 1912 National Coal which was basically a lost cause
3. 1919 Glasgow Shipbuilding agreed a 47 hour week.
4. 1931 Black Friday left Coal Miners with a partial temporary solution.
5. 1926 General Strike about how pay and poor conditions which then remained.
6. 1972 Coal Miners first strike since 1926 wage negotiations had collapsed and a state of emergency and 3 day working week followed. This was somewhat repeated in 1974 and probably caused the downfall of P.M. Edward Heath.
7. 1979 The Winter of Discontent was a result of demanding larger pay rises following Government attempts to cap pay. There followed a Maggie Thatcher landslide victory and legislation to restrict union powers was passed.
8. 1984 Coal Miners, but this did not stop pit closures and it was the beginning of the total demise of coal mining as a major industry.

This would indicate to me that in general, strikes do not give the floor worker a good return, as he gives up some of his regular pay and overtime to get a, relatively small, compensation from his union.

So how did we get to this situation? In the first instance the unions having convinced the workers that they had obtained a working relationship with the government, had a very high take up and arranged a number of closed shops. That meant that in all disputes or proposals for change they were the first and usually only port of call for negotiation. As I have said up until the 40s they appeared to be a clear element for the good. The problem came as the leaders of unions became, with the agreement of the management, full time workers for the union while being paid full time wages by the company. Why was this a problem, well, these people tasted power for the first time and as I see it, power begets power and total, power corrupts!

In order to retain power and to have their personal goals achieved it was necessary to get backing from the members for marginal decisions. As they were totally in charge they could call meetings for the members to vote at any time they felt was appropriate and often at very short notice. I think this position was abused and particularly in factories with 24 hour working shifts these meetings were convened to ensure minimum knowledge and minimum attendance. This enabled the senior activists to pass the word to selected members and ensure the required outcome. Am I a cynic? Yes!

Again it is only an opinion or feeling but the unions changed significantly after the Second World War and from clearly aiming at helping the lower classes they became an anti-capitalist anti royalist outfit.

Have I seen this through the wrong glasses? My memory tells me that the unions started to badger management for more of their profits to go towards pay increases and for them to reduce dividends. I am thinking particularly of Ford Dagenham where disputes and work to rule situations turned up regularly. I think after this had persisted for a number of years, most of the women working in the various factory areas, were all called out either on strike or insisted in working to rule., What really was this thing 'working to rule'? Well as referenced before the trade unions had over the years gained many benefits and working practices, including those related to working hours and these had been incorporated into the various companies' contracts with the workers. Working to rule was sticking inflexibly to these parts of the contract which in a lot of cases did not keep up with rate of change in production requirements. The unions tried to 'blackmail' companies into submission. In the case of Ford Dagenham which was American owned and had a number of factories in other parts of Europe they would not buckle and took their production elsewhere. Travelling down to Southend was never the same after that and felt like empty factories and laid off workers were the norm.

It would appear that a large proportion of the business population and their staff accepted that changes had and still should be made. Unfortunately there are three major unions who have a dominance for varied reasons and are influencing many wrong outcomes.

 The **NUT**, the teachers' union has a totally left wing attitude to life in general. Not necessarily a bad thing but it is used to indoctrinate upcoming teachers through the training colleges. Again where is the harm? Well, too simple really, the job of a teacher is to teach mostly a general education and not a personal belief. What I see is children being taught things like 'human rights', and being advised on how they can flout the law and argue with authority and their parents. Nowadays I see children leaving education not knowing the meaning of respect or responsibility and university students who seem to think it is their job to define the parameters when they are still in the process of learning. I said much earlier in these writings that a child did not appear to become an adult until they had passed significant milestones. Another side to this that I look for union support for change to assist Teachers to implement proper discipline into the classroom. Having taught the children their rights it would appear that the teachers have thereby forfeited their own rights and you would have hoped that the union could push for an improved situation. I think from what I have heard that the sole reason some teachers join the union is that a large majority advantage of the built in benefits (one in particular being Legal Costs). Back to classroom control; the union guarantee to support and pay court fees if and when they are sued by the children or their parents. This is a sticking plaster effect where the problem should be addressed at source. I think there are also other worthwhile attractive benefits for buying and club memberships. This large membership gives the union a lot of power and we have seen strikes which can only be to the detriment of education and the profession.

RMT the transport union is another dominant union although I cannot tell you why this is.

Arbitration became a legal requirement in the 80s but it would appear that not everybody understands arbitration in the same simple way. I have heard on many occasions one or the other side say that we have put our case and the arbitrator has not listened. What they are actually saying is that the arbitrator has stuck to his first analysis and they do not want to accept it. This of course is the whole purpose of arbitration in that they are required to make a rational decision where two parties have failed to come to an agreement. That should be end of story.

What we have seen in practice is that the RMT keep on going back to their members and encouraging them to take further industrial action in order to put pressure on the negotiations.

The RMT represent about 130 different union groups and in two ways they are apparently hypocritical. They agree a deal for one area and continue to fight it in another area. This is not democracy which they claim to stand for and secondly they wish to support the working class and argue against capitalism. Why then did Mr. Bob Crow the leader receive a massive remuneration in excess of £89,000 and, if rumours are true, also have resided in a four bed house in the country provided by the union for his lifetime.

In fact the RMT was not a union in its own rights until 1990 when it was created through a merger of the National Union of Railwayman (NUR) and the National Union of Seamen. It grew quickly and got a reputation of being regarded as one of, if not the, most radical trade union in Great Britain, able to organise massive industrial action within the transport industry especially the railway sector.

The RMT claims in its aims that protecting and bettering members pay and conditions are foremost. As an outsider and probably somewhat biased I translate the use of the protecting clause as being used to avoid any change when loss of jobs is identified as part of the improvements. I go back to the London Underground when driverless trains were developed and the union refused to let these run unless there was a driver and a guard on board. Today we are still arguing over the need for a guard in addition to the driver to monitor the computer controlled doors on mainline trains. It may be a fair debate but in some areas agreement has been reached whereas in others an industrial disruption is still occurring on a regular basis. I do not believe that this is really the proper member perceived focus for the union and that there are still many pay and condition variances that need their attention. I also understand that like the Teaching union they provide perks which are fairly comprehensive. They have their own finance company and provide a good life insurance for both staff and their families. These things boost the membership and give them disproportionate power through the internal democratic process (my opinion).

UNITE/UNISON. These are actually two separate unions but the patterns run parallel servicing either Public servants and contracted partners or public services like the NHS. Unison in particular derives its power from the fact it only became a union in 1993 when three existing unions merged:

NALGO National Government and Officers Association

NUPE National Union of Public Employees

COHSE Confederation of Health Service Employees

UNISON now consists of mainly National Health Service Local Government and the Police and is made up of Porters/Nurses/Ambulance crew/clerical/Therapists. Now in the 2000s it is one of the most aggressive unions and is often threatening strike action.

Going back in history probably the most prominent of the three unions in the NHS was COHSE and they were to the forefront in the 1970s. Prior to this time industrial action of any kind in the NHS was rare. As the new decade dawned, tensions that had been building over a period of years came to a head, together with increasing social unrest across the country a series of strikes affecting every level of the NHS took place. These strikes had an element of success in that they encouraged a lot of discussion and prompted some significant re-evaluation. However after an action lasting six weeks and affecting 300 hospitals I wonder if we should not be able, particularly in a critical service, to get the same results in a more professional manner. After the 1973 strike according to a hospital porter in London and a steward with NUPE 'the strike itself was no great victory, but it changed the way workers felt. At the end of the strike... he a cleaner who hadn't had a mop in three years got one. The porters got a fridge in their restroom. Now, nobody could be fired out of hand because their face didn't fit'

The 1974 strike did not fit comfortably with the nurses but their plight was looked at sympathetically and a parliamentary committee awarded them a considerable pay rise based on about a million letters of public support.

Even into the 2000s there are still strikes and threats of strikes on a regular basis and I am sure that by now you understand that I think there is a good reason to have a union and for the workers to have input directly to management. I also think that discussion and arbitration should prevail and if this fails maybe the courts should get involved. I did read somewhere that one of the unions has created a guide to striking workers advising that they keep a good diary as all strikes have elements that are against the law. I will close on unions with a note that I was saddened when I discovered the British Medical Association, it seems, is now actually a full time union.

CHAPTER ELEVEN

THE POLICE FORCE

I know that the force was started by Peel and that they were called the Peelers. I am, however, concerned with the 1900s. At the beginning of my review the regular bobby was literally the man on the beat. We are in an era before telephones, walkie-talkies and indeed mobile phones. The bobby was your neighbourhood friendly visitor. He, and it was at that time, always a he, who was always close on six foot tall.

The local copper had a regular beat that he pounded most of his eight hour shift and because of this you could usually get hold of him if needed, quite quickly. If he was needed elsewhere for any reason he had the old fashioned police box at various points on his journey's round the neighbourhood, which if the blue light flashed meant he had to call in to the station. He could also use these boxes if he needed backup.

In general policing was limited to things like burglaries, shoplifting, moving on vagrants, booking drunkards and prostitutes and stopping kids riding bikes on the pavement. In fact the first role of the police was to:

Patrol the streets

Deter criminals

Investigate crimes

Arrest suspects.

This was actually supplemented by the knowledge he gained about the people and the district, which meant that he was also noting things like child abuse and genuine poverty.

The turn of the century saw lots of additional responsibilities being passed on to the local police with the progress of life styles, particularly noticeable with the emergence of motor cars and the related regulations.

I am not sure but think that in the twenties the police got used to handling picket line disputes and other pockets of disorder.

Going back to 1900 there were 45,800 police in England, Wales and Scotland and in the year 2000 there were 125,000 officers and in1970 there were 91,000. (These numbers seem to show that although often claimed otherwise in the press the police were not understaffed at the turn of the century in 2000).

Now for my bit of history as per the records. During the First World War the police became unionised. The Police Act of 1919 was passed in response to the police striking. It criminalised the police union, replacing it with the Police Federation of England and Wales. This act also guaranteed a pension for police; previously it had been discretionary. In 1923 the Special Constables Act throughout the UK was passed. The1946 Police Act abolished almost all non-county borough police forces in England and Wales. 1964 saw the number of police forces reduced from over 100 to 49 and some of these covered two or more counties or large urban areas. 1974 these were reduced to 43.

!977 identified corruption at the Flying Squad with a conviction of a Detective Chief Superintendent.

1989The West Midlands Serious Crime Squad was disbanded as around 100 criminal cases failed or were overturned in the West Midlands, as it was shown that statement evidence had been tampered to secure convictions. (There appears to be a similar failure with the presentation of evidence in Financial Fraud Squad cases and significant shortcomings within the CPS, in recent years).

1999 the MacPherson report describes the Metropolitan Police Service as 'institutionally racist'.

So much for the modernisation of the police forces during the 1900s!

I will now return to my youth and confirm that at that time the police were well respected and known as totally honest by upright citizens. If you were stopped by one policeman then there was a chance that you would get a clip round the ear and a warning with a threat that he would come round and tell your dad. You did not want this or to tell your father what had happened as the nett result in either case was a further clip from your father at a minimum. On occasions there were two policemen and if you upset them and they wanted to take the problem further, you had no chance because two coppers were always thought to be honest and you were in the wrong. I must say this was probably true in at least 90% of the cases. I referenced earlier that we were advised via pop music that 'things ain't what they used to be'. Well with the police this is very true and to some degree I wish their job could go back to basics.

From Bobbies on the beat they progressed to Velocette motorcycles and then they retreated into the confines of police cars with blues and twos (the blue and red flashing lights and the double horn). When the riots started in Brixton the police started to go round in twos to protect themselves not to improve crime detection and arrest. The police for many reasons seemed to lose credibility over the years and by the late 1990s the general public often had the opinion that the police hunted in twos in order to collude and ensure a conviction. Probably not true as I still think at least 95% of the population are actually totally honest, but the odd bad egg leaves a bad smell.

How did this all come about, well, police were given menial tasks which were easy to handle and seen by the public as unnecessary and often over zealously implemented. Let me see, it started with things like speeding fines without a caution but a straight ticket and moved on through all the various motoring offences, no Tax disc or insurance (you must present them within seven days at the local police station or face prosecution) and then social misdemeanours and domestic problems. They appeared no longer to be doing the job expected of them and stopped attending break-ins at the house then only visited a motor accident if there was at least a serious injury, (although they did provide an incident number for the insurance claim). When they did attend they became so frightened of repercussions, from the public and insurance companies, that they closed roads and spent endless hours measuring and calculating to have sufficient evidence if a court case ensued. The traffic jams that occurred clearly did not please the busy car driver. I do not think the police liked this progress and the morale dropped and this only made things worse. In the early eighties in order to create a more inclusive policing the Neighbourhood Watch was created to get people to look out for each other and to meet regularly with the local constabulary appointed officer. They also increasingly focused on crime prevention and each force now has a Crime Prevention Officer who visits schools and attends community meetings. Technology has progressed dramatically and there are number plate recognition cameras everywhere to record the cars presence on the road but this does not automatically connect to the DVLA so that they can trap untaxed and uninsured drivers on an immediate basis. One must assume that the liberal community has got involved and advised that this type of action would impede on human rights. The regular motorist does not want to finish up having an accident with an untaxed uninsured driver because of the extra hassle nor does he enjoy paying an element of his insurance to cover this kind of accident which is currently included in standard cover.

I have an outlandish theory that with all the emphasis on education through to your eighteenth birthday we could actually do away with driving schools and add driving into the regular school curriculum. This would free up quite a large workforce (Driving schools and instructors) who could be employed as a form of highway patrol that stopped drivers for real offences and had immediate feedback to hand held technology from national computer centres. If we then stopped the police handling domestic problems and limited their social interface to what went on in the community and the schools, we could perhaps once again have a proper police force. They would be able to follow up on shoplifting and burglary among other things already within their remit. It was also once the case the policeman could complete an arrest right through to the courts. We now to feed everything through the CPS to see if a prosecution is appropriate. This has been far from fool proof and prosecutions have failed because of lack of proper evidence or simply lack of the correct paperwork, arranged attendance of relevant witnesses, or 'experts'. Maybe it is time to re-think the process and cut the time and procedural steps it takes to come to court. Get rid of the Crown Prosecution Service and let the police, police!

CHAPTER TWELVE

CHARITIES

Charities have been about since 597 when the first charity, King's School, Canterbury was established, and it is still in existence to this day. It was not, until, in 1853 that, The Charities Commission was established under the Charitable Trusts Act. Not a lot has changed since then but it is worth noting

1916 The Police, Factories etc. Act requires a charity to obtain a licence for charitable collections.

1939 The House to House Collections Act passed specific regulations for this activity.

1960 The Charities Act introduced the registration of all charities and gave the Charity Commission powers of investigation.

1992 The Charities Act introduced compulsory registration for all charities with an income of over £1000 and also brought in new regulations for fundraising. At this point I seem to be implying that charity is a form of collection for the good of others. In truth early charities were often concerned with education and providing bursaries to the less fortunate. All private schools would I suspect have applied for charitable status to obtain the tax and ancillary benefits. The Charity Commission has a statement 'To ensure charity can thrive and inspire trust so that people can improve lives and strengthen society'

Their 5 strategic objectives are:

Holding charities to account.

Dealing with wrongdoing and harm

Informing public choice

Giving charities the understanding and tools they need to succeed.

Keeping charity relevant for today's world.

It would seem that by the early 2000s a charity could be almost all things to all people and in modern parlance the definition of a charity is:

An institution which both:

Is established for charitable purposes.

Falls under the control of the high court in the exercise and jurisdiction with respect to charities

A charitable purpose is one of the following purposes which is for public benefit.

The prevention or relief of poverty.

The advancement of education.

The advancement of religion.

The advancement of health and the saving of lives.

The advancement of citizenship and community development.

The advancement of the arts, culture, heritage or science.

The advancement of amateur sport.

The advancement of human rights, conflict resolution reconciliation, or the promotion of religious or racial harmony or equality and diversity.

The advance of environmental protection or improvement.

The relief of those in need by reason of youth, disability, age, ill-health, financial hardship or other disadvantage.

The advancement of animal welfare.

The promotion of the efficiency of the armed forces of the Crown or the efficiency of the police, fire and rescue services or ambulance services.

Certain further purposes, including any that may reasonably be regarded as analogous to or within the spirit of those listed.

The Charity Commission has wide ranging powers and with the equally wide ranging definition of what constitutes a charity it seems that my early comments regarding trying to amend your role to reflect your personal opinion can come into force here. By applying a broad interpretation on what a particular charity is supposed to provide gives a free ticket to the Charity Commission to provide its own interpretation of what is a misdemeanour. This appeared to be the case when the commission publically sought to take charity status away from public schools. The court decided that it was not who provided the funds for them to support a fulfilling education but the fact that they gave bursaries to rich and poor alike and supported, in many cases, also accepted pupils from local state schools, evidenced why they deserved charitable status.

This presentation of the change in charity organisations during the 1900s will be based on my own personal reflections. During the war we used to walk to the local church on a Sunday morning and always walked past a beggar just below the green below the church and I guess this was my first experience of what or who needed charity. At Christmas we as kids would prance along the road towards the poor man and sing:

Christmas is coming, the goose is getting fat

Please do put a penny in the old man's hat

If you haven't a penny a halfpenny will do

If you haven't a halfpenny God bless you!

After the war charity, I realised, was more commercialised and the government allocated several days a year to charity days. I remember Queen Elizabeth day, and poppy day particularly but there were others. I also know that bonfire nights started to make collections for local causes or in some cases were themselves a local charity.

Around the early 1950s the first really big charity I was aware of was OXFAM. All of a sudden people were knocking on your door and trying to sell you football pontoon tickets. These cost about 6d each and you had a chance of winning quite a lot of money. It was not long before I also found out that the tickets were sold by the equivalent of door-to-door salesmen. First they received payment for selling the tickets which destroyed my idea of what charity really was. I always thought these people were volunteers and time was given for free. Worse came when I found out that this was in essence a business and that less than 5% of the money collected actually contributed to the stated purpose of the charity, the rest went on administration (mostly salaries).

Fast forward a number of years and all the empty shops on the High streets were becoming charity shops. Again in my ignorance I thought that as these were temporarily empty and they were occupied by the charities on a no rent basis. Wrong again, they had paid managers and a mixture of volunteer and paid staff. You have to be very aware today as to whether you are giving that all your contribution goes to the cause of the charity or you are lining the pockets of overpaid directors and staff. Worse still, going back to my comments about corruption and fraud it has been recognised that in many instances helpers travelling abroad to help on things like famine relief, have in truth stayed in 5 star hotels and in some cases taken sexual advantage of the locals.

I will not name the charities that I will not give to but I will say that at all levels there are still genuine worthwhile causes. In the RNLI and many mountain and cave rescue teams give all their time for free and there are small charities like the one that I was president of, where none of the committee or ancillary members take a penny and getting the few thousand pound per year we needed often cost a lot of time, dedication and expense. Never a complaint as it was more than a worthwhile return seeing the benefits. It would be great if we could return to this real charity but the whole thing has gone worldwide and in the case of national disasters there is even a central charity that co-ordinates the giving of various associated charities.

Needless to say the do-gooders and lobbyists have got in on the act and convinced the government to produce a product called 'GIFT AID'. This sounds like the best thing since sliced bread to the charities and their dedicated donors. I, as usual, have a different take on this. If I give £100 to my favourite charity then fill in a gift aid form they will receive a further £20 from the Inland Revenue, ostensibly from my tax payments. The truth is that all of these payments have to be covered by the Inland Revenue collecting a matching sum of money to compensate. I do not and will not think this makes good sense when putting on my business hat.

Do I believe in Charity, Yes desperately! I do not believe in the commercialisation of it. The local small cancer hospitals seemed to be getting along quite well up to the early 90s but too many now employ professional fundraisers. There must be a better way to provide these necessary facilities!

CHAPTER THIRTEEN

LAW

Britain has always been respected the world over and when I started work in the 50s virtually every trading contract regardless of Country of origin or destination, finished up with a comment like 'if all else fails the dispute will be resolved in the British Courts'. This was the result of the reputation of our law for being totally unbiased and incorruptible.

Prior to the Norman Conquest in 1066, there was no unitary, national legal system. The law has developed along two separate lines, that of the Criminal Law and that of the Common Law. There have always been different levels of administration from local to national administration and we have local magistrates, justices of the peace, travelling crown courts, the crown high court, the Supreme Court and pretty well at the top, yes, the House of Lords. And until the introduction of the court of human rights and the European court of appeal (after our entry into the common market) this was it. Criminal law has developed through local law and in the early days it came under the King's jurisdiction when the first national circuit judges travelled the country to administer a common law. It was also the beginnings of building up the reputation of our courts for giving honest outcomes. The use of local dignitary as judges had apparently seen a high element of corruption which the new system managed to effectively overcome. Juries were re-introduced and the actions of the courts were formally recorded.

Step forward a few hundred years and most of our laws were then created in parliament which was now seen to be good, as it was constituted of our regularly elected countrywide members of that parliament. This mainly relates to Criminal Law but does sometimes overflow into the Common Law. Most of Common Law has however been built up from the records that have been kept and then used in the courts as precedent. The Common Law has at times been referred to as the Law of Precedent. The different levels of the law has created a system whereby if you feel hard done by in a lower court you can be given leave to apply to a higher court to reverse the decision. This could always proceed as far as The House of Lords if thought appropriate. Alongside Precedents and juries a third law was enacted. The Doctrine of the Supremacy of the Law. Originally, supremacy of the law meant that not even the king was above the law; today it means that acts of government agencies and ministers can be challenged in the courts.

All of this development has been exemplary but the comments recently of a law student 'in recent decades it has been somewhat undermined by the increase in judicial activism in making and interpreting the law, and by increasing the influence of European Union jurisprudence since the UK's joining the Community'. I made this point earlier and I feel that there have been cases where groups or individuals with enough money have challenged parliamentary decisions and, I think, obtained very controversial outcomes passed by very liberal and possibly biased senior judges. This goes back to my earlier comments regarding people looking for personal recognition, dare I say, quotes on the front pages of the press.

Even worse is that this liberalism has crept down into the lower courts right down to the local magistrate courts. We are seeing reduced sentences based on the upbringing of the defendant (had they been abused or deprived?). This extends into many more areas now and includes racism, sexual orientation, climate change even possibly personal profiles. Jail sentences have on average become shorter, or even deferred, and the quality of life inside the jail is now often a better standard than the incumbent has been used to on the outside. We have charities supporting the inmates while the wardens are, at times, unable to keep control and certainly do not seem to have the will or powers to prevent drugs being brought into the prisons and to stop the inmates from carrying on their criminal activities using mobile phones.

At this point a little light relief may come from this short anecdote of what I overheard on a local train in the mid-80s. People used to travel in little groups in their own part of the train and you got to know where the interesting chatting took place and homed in on this instead of trying to complete the 'Telegraph' crossword puzzle of the man next to you. Anyway a young girl that had not been in the group for several weeks turned up. The first reaction of the rest of her friends was 'what was it like'? And her response was it was comfortable and better than being cooped up at home with mum and dad and having no choice on what was on the telly. In fact I was really well off except that I could not go clubbing at the weekend. She had apparently been 'unfortunate' enough to have been serving a short prison sentence but seemed happy that if it only happened once a year it was as good as a holiday. Are the hard working upright members of the population now having to live as if they are the lower class citizens?

Other intrusions into the law here have been impacted by changes across the pond i.e. America. The most significant change, in my mind, is the introduction of the compensation generation. Back to my childhood I remember that when someone made a mistake it was enough to make an appropriate apology and life went on. Today it would appear that there is no such thing as a mistake or an accident. In every case today the thing anyone says is 'you will claim compensation, won't you'. This is of course right in a number of incidences where the problem was a result of incompetence, neglect or deliberately ignoring basic rules and regulations e.g. health and safety. I truly believe that there are many areas where compensation should not be considered. I am thinking particularly of professionals going about their work to the best of their ability at that time. In this category, right at the top of the list, are doctors, nurses, police, fireman and what I think I am saying is that an accident is an accident and the mistake is sufficient to impact the person who made the mistake for the rest of their life. Monetary payment to the person who in essence has lost nothing as they knew of the risk and were certainly not expecting to have a better life style but only hopefully some change or improvement, is out of order. We have inherited what was, in America, labelled as Ambulance Chasers where legal companies offered to make a compensation claim after an accident for no fee but a % of any settlement. This was seen as moral as it was believed that an insurance company would cover the cost. This then extended to things like miss-selling, which was or was not an intentional fraud, but was certainly the best deal for the buyer. Again real miss-selling should be punished but giving money and an overgenerous interest payment to someone who had been totally happy and content with the arrangement is out of order. We have lost any semblance of sense and responsibility and given way to greed base on human rights or some such excuse. We will not be able to stop people believing they have a claim that they say has impacted their way of living and wellbeing. I however think that the professions and professional bodies and public services should be legally exempt from fractious claims but only be held responsible under current criminal law.

I know that this is and will continue to be a contentious issue but the Hillsborough football stadium disaster was exactly that. Nobody made a conscious or sub-conscious decision to create a situation that would cause death or destruction. Who should pay for the outcome of this tragic accident? Well we are back to the ambulance chasers who believe that there is usually some insurance company in the background. I am sure this is true and appropriate compensation, where appropriate, could be claimed. Random shootings and other tragedies can fall into this category.

That does it for law and order but let me just say that I still think that the courts should be in charge and we should stop allowing unelected bodies to impose fines; please let the courts resume this responsibility. Yes I know there is a perceived need for government overview (watchdogs) and if necessary we should create bodies to oversee good practice but if a misdemeanour is found, it should go to the courts.

That includes compensation and related claims within traditional laws. We do not need the new-fangled human rights laws when the basics are already cared for in existing law.

CHAPTER FOURTEEN

BANKING

Banking does not have a simple chronological progression of laws like much of commerce. Banking has been very evolutionary and progressed from bartering to money lending and currency exchange with various laws relating to things like cheques and bills of exchange.

Cheques came in to existence about two hundred years ago or more and were originally only cashable within a few miles of where they were issued. This evolved to such a degree that a clearing house was set up in London which met daily and was based on money changing hands at the beginning and end of each day. A similar clearing ran alongside this in other large towns and it can be argued that Birmingham had an effective clearing before London. By the turn of the twentieth century there was a countrywide General clearing based in London with Metropolitan clearing systems in local towns and boroughs and even smaller clearing between banks situated within cycling distance of each other. Before I go on to bills of exchange I remember reading a quote in a text book which described banking as legalised fraud. This is not an unreasonable comment as the basis of banking within the law allowed banks to borrow and lend money over various periods of time but either leave items in transit or run a pay later policy. Let me explain that if you opened a bank account the bank did not mind if you wrote a cheque for £100 or went overdrawn by £100. These actions both within themselves created profit; the cheque was passed to a third party and did not return to be cleared for at least several days and in the meantime the bank could put the £100 out on loan and earn interest, in the case of the overdraft they would simply earn interest at an agreed rate. In addition to the cheque system the banks could make loans over say 7, 21, 30, or 90 days and let the settlements overlap which meant they appeared to lend the money six or seven times over. The rationale for this was that at any one time only one eighth of monies would be required at short notice and therefore the remainder could be lent out. This theory of not being required repeated itself over the various extended periods. If an individual tried to do this it would definitely be classed as fraud.

The banks had started life much earlier as merchant bankers in the original sense of the word. They funded merchants when they moved their goods to a buyer and collected the money when the merchant received his payment. This method was formalised under law in the Bills of Exchange Act 1882. This also grew into a foreign exchange market as imports and exports to other countries became popular. In this case the banks probably made money both on the delay interest and also a turn on the foreign exchange transaction. This really summarises banking until at least the end of the Second World War.

In fact I started work in the foreign branch of a British bank in London in 1954 and it was during the latter part of my seven years that banking started to change. In London particularly an excessive number of American banks had opened alongside at least one from most other major countries of the world. Around 1960 the American banks started to amalgamate in the states and this led to a number of them having more than one representative office in London but although they closed some facilities they expanded dramatically in staff numbers and services. I took this opportunity to leave my 'dead man's' shoes career and take my chance with progress. First I must say that where I worked the business was also changing and where foreign exchange was traditionally a service to our customers in support of their business needs they were now developing a foreign exchange trading desk. This meant that in what appeared to go against the articles of association which did not allow them to put their customer's monies at risk, they were now gambling on a daily basis.

The American banks were in fact the forerunners of the modern Merchant Bank. They chased certain industries for their custom with specialist support management. Particularly things like oil and shipping but also major manufacturers' in heavy industry like aeroplanes and automobiles. These companies tried at one stage to set up their own foreign exchange trading desks but I think it was a major motor car company in France that were taken to court and advised that it was not in their remit to run this kind of risk business, and the banks retained dominance. The term merchant seems now to more reflect the activity of the bank and not its customer.

The idea of extending banking to a new and more profitable business took off and from providing better cash flow through a new swap system (converting half yearly/yearly dividend type income into monthly to match business needs) actually trading in swapping monies on a created market. These markets could be straight money deals or could exchange packets of commodities with a long term value for an immediate cash input to the customer's account. In Canada in the 70s some banks bought packages of mortgages which when the market failed put them into severe difficulty. Governments and Banks got into severe cash flow problems and both Hungary and South America trading desks had to be sorted out. At this time the World's banking community handled the problem and jointly arranged a steady and satisfactory administration. This was not to be handled as well in the early 2000s but that is a much later story.

Banking appeared to get carried away with the ease in which it could create markets and in turn create money and profits. It believed the boffins who were running the trading area and paid them good money but also started to pay commission up front for long term deals where the real profit or loss came at maturity. Some of these dealers moved on before the potential problem and others saw their own problems and started to gamble and or manipulate the market rates. Again the story is not in my domain as far as my time slot is concerned. The banks also started to sell insurance alongside mortgages and although the customer liked the product and cost it turned out that in many cases they had miss-sold related insurance and the comeuppance was refunds with interest. This new style merchant or investment banking has a lot to answer for and I still think that it has developed where the shareholders did not insist that the articles of association were abided by; gambling should have been shot in the bud. We have the same age old problem though; that these same shareholders were very happy to gain the high returns that had started to accrue.

In the meantime the domestic banking system moved steadily forward and although many will tell you otherwise this country has always provided free banking to any customer who wanted it. The press and customers who wanted to live on permanent credit have argued that they are being ripped off. I think that if you strike an agreement with someone then you should stick by it. When you think you can simply go over an agreed overdraft without 'a by your leave or may I' do not at the same time expect it not to cost you. If you allowed your child to have a credit card you would not expect them to use it to a degree that they overdrew their allowance and left you to pay the costs. It sounds more drastic in the limited environment of a family but the principle is no different. I believe that a sensible deterrent should be in place at all times to stop petty abuse. It is unfortunately a fact of life that change occurs and in banking the development of computerisation, and particularly proliferation of debit and credit cards, footfall has fallen in the smaller branches out in the country which means that many will close. Let us hope that the banking community can come up with a solution to providing the comprehensive service the customer would like. Some suggest that the imminence of the cashless society will solve all our problems.

CHAPTER FIFTEEN

INSURANCE

I am sure that with most people the first thing we think of when we talk about the history of Insurance is Lloyds of London. I am going to go back a lot further to possibly medieval times when the word insurance had probably not been part of the vocabulary. Merchants would ply their trade in foreign lands and send loaded ships across the oceans packed with goods for sale. The savvy moneylenders thought up the idea of guaranteeing that if the ship flailed and did not return they would, for a certain consideration, provide the wherewithal for a replacement. As the length of time between the transaction and the possible payment the process was a simple interest calculation based how much and how many months were involved. The capital from the premium would then earn the cost of the pay out or hopefully a bit more. If the ship returns both parties are very happy. Very much later after the great fire of London in 1666 a market started up in fire insurance.

Back to Lloyds of London this was based also on marine insurance and developed in a coffeehouse in or near the corn exchange in the City of London. This establishment was patronised by merchants, bankers, and insurance underwriters for marine insurance. Edward Lloyd supplied his customers with shipping information gathered in the docks and other sources; this eventually grew into the publication Lloyds List, still in existence. Lloyd's was recognised in 1769 as a formal group of underwriters accepting marine risks. With the growth of British sea power, Lloyd's became the dominant insurer of marine risks, to which were later added fire and other property risks. Today Lloyd's is a major reinsurer as well as a primary insurer, but it does not itself transact insurance business; this is done by the member underwriters, who accept insurance on their own account and bear the full risk of competition with each other. Note: the word underwriter is said to have derived from the practice of having each risk taker write his name under the total amount of risk that he was willing to accept at a specified premium.

On this basis insurance is a straight calculation of premium based on risk. In fact this is quite complex and a whole business of Actuary was developed to support the industry.

These people worked out things like life expectancy, type and severity of possible claims in fire and motor accidents and factored in costs or earnings of monies over the term of insurance.

As I have referred to previously in the 60s, after the McKinsey report, statistics and actions became the measuring points for all business activities. This did not, at the time, seem to seriously impact the way insurance premiums were calculated, but as time passed the politically correct forum got in on the act and encouraged significant change.

In the latter part of the 1900s instead of genuine risk being the basis for calculating cost of cover it was deemed, at times, more important to consider things like equality and public interests. At first it was a simple feminist male/female considerations but before I start being opinionated about this aspect I will address the earlier scandal, if that is what it really was, of miss selling mortgage/endowment polices. When I bought my first house I took out an endowment policy to ensure that if within the 25 years of the policy I happened to die, then the remaining outstanding debt would be paid out in full. Additionally if I had not needed to use the policy as life insurance then I would have accrued, through the annual bonuses etc. a cash payment at maturity. This did actually work and was significantly to my benefit. Many years later the banks sold endowment polices for terms as short as five years. This both did not give the time for the system to grow and was unable to necessarily cope with sudden drops in interest rates which had always been fairly managed for long term policies. The press caught on to the fact that people who believed these policies gave them full protection were in fact coming up short. The insurance companies became the scapegoat but this was the press jumping on the publicity bandwagon. It was true that the expected monies were not available but this was more likely to be a case of miss selling by the banks than policies not providing promised outcomes. At this time the 25 year polices were still giving more than satisfactory returns. This tells me that the system of using actuaries did in fact work.

Back to political correctness and an early example of directives from government bodies was that in the case of motor insurance the practice of assessing policy prices on evidenced risk should be ignored and men and women should pay a similar cost for similar cover. Different but just as relevant is that because of postcodes playing a key role you can now live at the top of a hill and have your premium raised because of local subsidence, surely unless this is the source of a spring or river there is no possibility of subsidence which has been added to the costs. Sports clubs were in some cases refused certain liability insurance unless the committee had appointed a specific officer for Child Protection and Vulnerable Adults and had rules in place to cover the transport of boys and girls up to the age of eighteen to ensure proper segregation and supervision by appropriate mix of relevant male and female supervisors. It had always been a requirement that quality health and safety rules were in place and adhered to but when the smoking ban came in more questions were raised and restrictions and costs were blamed on, perhaps, not being able to obtain insurance. The same happened with laws and climate control where premiums could be varied according to a company's carbon footprint. Insurance, like many other things had become more of a tick box application applied to apply a premium rather than a risk assessment. Pensions and life related insurances required you to list all of your ailments and illnesses but after a time these were apparently simply entered into a computer which made a cold decision to allow or reject cover, and no discounts were allowed for pensions or life cover in the major companies to be made on a group risk but each member of the fund was either treated individually or the group all assumed to be going to live to an annually adjusted average length of life. No special consideration for vulnerable groups or the very fit! As with the banks, insurance used to employ staff straight from school and train them to a professional standard, but now the majority of young staff are not there for a career and are mainly people willing to work for a minimum wage and want fixed short hours per week so they can in my quotes 'enjoy life'. I guess at this point you might be saying that I should move with the times. Maybe but I still think some things have come too far too fast.

CHAPTER SIXTEEN

ACCOUNTING

This follows a similar pattern to Banking and Insurance, so I will address government involvement in the auditing of Boards of Directors, their make-up, and directives with regards to the management of pension funds.

Let me start off with the board of Directors; the lack of equality and the overwhelming dominance of all male board's was perceived as an unacceptable situation, and public opinion was apparently strong enough for the government to pass specific directives that were intended to ensure that boards' would eventually be split evenly between the sexes. Even many years later there are still a lot of men only boards but in the top footsie companies female representation is growing but, not so, it would appear, at the top level of the actual board appointments.

It was also felt that boards were too dominant and reflected the personal opinions of the grey haired old men that had had full control for many years. This had to be addressed, in order to satisfy statisticians and the press in particular, that things were properly thought through and given independent scrutiny. To ensure this, boards of larger and more important companies, were directed to appoint executive directors who would have the power to influence, as necessary, the actions of the board. From where I see it this has not actually turned out as expected and there are now a number of Ex Directors and M P's appointed and many have taken on well paid, limited attendance commitments, for several companies. I have not heard of any significant positive results. Companies have customers and shareholders to bring them to account and I do not think that arbitrary directives from government is what we voted them in to exact.

The government at the same time as changing the tax on pension investment also made a change to the rules regarding total funds values versus anticipated future drawdowns. It had always been the accountants along with the actuaries who valued pensions for viability. This apparently all had to change when a couple of significant company failures highlighted shortfalls in the pension reserves. As has become common these problems were front page news and it was therefore beholding on the government to address what was now perceived as a problem. Most companies who had a final salary pension had the portfolio fully reviewed on a biennial or five yearly basis with reviews at each annual audit of the fund. In most cases this was seen to be working. The chancellor in his wisdom pronounced that, considering the shortcomings identified, that he would need to use a sledge hammer to crack the proverbial nut. He decided that the whole valuation process should be done monthly and that at all times the reserves should more than enough to cover the potential outgoings in the long term. This is not how the consultants advised the public on stock market investments as they preached that values could go up as well as down and that a personal portfolio should be treated on five year cycles. Pension funds all incorporated rules to ensure a mixed investment to spread risk and avoid fluctuations. If this was true for you and me then why should big business be encumbered with additional monthly accounting and reporting and the government controllers' be given significant extra responsibilities and therefore require more staff to monitor these funds on a virtually daily basis. With automatic computer systems already both buying and selling in order to maintain safe agreed ratios this added review appears only to succeed in costing the funds administrative expenses in continually encouraging them to re-assess risk and maybe take greater risks to retain values without having to go to the board for additional funds. I am finding this far too complicated to explain and feel that this reflects my opinion of what happens when tick boxing statistics come into force, that is, more low standard working practices and less, good experienced management.

CHAPTER SEVENTEEN

ECONOMICS

I have named this chapter economics although as you will already appreciate, other than when I talk budgets I seem to treat economics as statistics.

I will now explain the history of this and trust you will see my point. In about 1954 the education system was expanding and more university degrees were being invented. There was an open discussion in the press at that time as to whether the new economics degree should be introduced as an art or a science degree. At my school we found the topic of particular interest and it was always my opinion that it was an art. The reasoning behind this was that sciences should always have a proven, basically indisputable, answer to equations or prognosis. Mathematics, Chemistry, Physics, Biology etc. were subjects where you felt that at the end of any problem, project or thesis could always be finished off with the letters QED (Quod Erat Demontrandum). This translates loosely to mean that which has been demonstrated or therefore proven. From what I had gleaned from the business pages of the newspapers was that these new-fangled economists could not actually prove anything but were giving an opinion based on numbers and historical trends. QED they are not scientists.

I thought this was bad at that time but with the passage of time and a lot of evolution statistics has taken over pretty well completely. Today we do not just have an extrapolation of figures varied by personal bias we have created the belief that although the results of surveys and polls are real they are not real for the statistician. They decide that the mix or locality of the base input was not reflective of the environment that they wish to review and therefore find the need to factor in adjustments. They create percentage variations for things like population mix, class, ethnic origins, quality of life and in fact anything which gives the analyst the opportunity to show the figures support the result he was looking for in the first place. You might think that I am being harsh but sometimes you see a poll of less than 100 participants taken on a single website with the results telling us that so many thousands in so many million are to be effected in a particular manner. We also get advised that we have so many cases of asthma or diabetes or whatever that has n thousands of sufferers who have no symptoms but are still out there to be counted anyway. Enough said.

CHAPTER EIGHTEEN

EDUCATION

This chapter may give me a preview of how I will proceed in Book Two which will investigate natural progression in developments in science and technology. In schools around 1900 early learning in starter schools introduced the young children into handwriting using sand trays. The child could copy a letter and then simply shake the tray to smooth it ready to write another letter. This learning to write progressed to a slate and pencil which was cleaned regularly with a soapy damp towel or, to a messy white chalk and board which when cleaned created a fearful mess which could get all over the children's clothes, often creating trouble, particularly for the girls when they got home. Real progress was made after this when paper and dip-in pens and ink were introduced. (The only real progress was that you got a hard copy to be marked by the teacher in his/her own time and it could be taken home for the parents to criticise). This in truth meant that the desks had to have a special hole to house an inkwell, which had to be cleaned and filled regularly, and a slot to stop the pen from rolling off. The pen itself was quite fragile and you had to insert a nib into a holder in order to use it. These nibs were fairly weak especially when handled by a child and therefore were forever having to be replaced, but that was only the beginning as you were not expected to drip ink when taking the pen from the inkwell to the paper and you were not expected to drip ink all over the desk and your clothing. Welcome the next step forward, which in this case, was a true improvement. This was the fountain pen which had a rubber reservoir to hold enough ink for at least a day's work and would let the ink flow evenly to give a pleasant clean finish. We then go backwards to the ballpoint pen that was actually cheap and effective but not as permanent and definitely not so well presented as a final article. Most teachers did not think this was the way to go but as with a lot of things, convenience got the better of quality, and until computers were introduced the ballpoint pen prevailed.

Let us now look at how the schools themselves progressed. In the early 1900s the downside was that lots of schools had classes of around 60 pupils and the upside that there were some very good design features. Some schools had tiered seating in the classrooms much like the end of century lecture and laboratory layouts. This enabled the teacher to see all the individual pupils from their position at the front of the classroom. (A definite plus when compared to the later part of the 1900s when kids could hide behind each other and their desks to avoid attention). The teachers were not encouraged to go round the class behind each child and look over their shoulder but rather to sit quietly at the front of the room giving instruction. The teacher was given a position of authority by being seated on a high stool with a high desk. As mentioned earlier teachers, by the late 1900s, seemed to have lost the ability and the tools to gain the respect of the pupils. The simple practice of dressing properly for the occasion and being given an air of being in charge by being in a position of dominance seemed to work. I cannot say that this control was solely the person and their status or how much it was supplemented by corporal punishment which was handed out fairly liberally.

Schooling and classes did not change much until after the Second World War and my first school pretty well resembled the ones of the early 1900s. The schools were either single sex or were generally segregated within, often having the youngest, maybe mixed, on the ground floor with the girls on the first floor and the boys on the top floor. There were separate playgrounds with toilets in each. Mostly meals were not provided and the kids either took a sandwich or went home for the dinner break (lunch time). Further education was mainly for the rich and in the towns where families tended to be quite large the first school leavers in the household were immediately sent out to work to help dad out with the cost of rearing the youngsters. Mothers in general did not go out to work so money was often tight. My own mother left school at around 14 and started work in a brush factory and in her case, although not the eldest, acquired the job of running the household as her father was away from home. The younger children did at times get a chance to further their education but any advancement was generally achieved through evening classes. What was also clear in those days was that the basic school day included extra curricula such as physical recreation, maybe swimming or singing and particularly cricket, football and rounders. The teachers were apparently also happy to stay extra hours to coach budding sportspersons. Sunday school played a big part in the children's education because if a child attended a minimum number of meetings they would be eligible for a free coach trip to the coast or maybe a visit to a pantomime at Christmas. Some children managed to play the system and get more than one outing by going to different Sunday Schools without a care as to what the religion was, but this surely went on, as my parent's generation were particularly well versed in the teachings of the bible.

After the Second World War, after the NHS, education was a major topic. My elder brother was born in 1935 and was one of the very first to take the 11 plus examination and also in the last year of matriculation. To matriculate at the age of sixteen one had to take at least five subjects and pass five subjects at the one go to gain a pass. The 11 plus was brought in immediately after the war and was the first time selection for the next level of schooling was considered. This exam rated all 11 year old's upon the result of this single exam which was taken in their last year at primary school. You either passed or failed. If you passed you could select three Grammar schools that you would like to attend, in order of preference, and although you were allocated one of these, there was, I seem to remember, an entry interview. If you were off school sick at the date fixed for the exam there was then a later date for you available after you had recovered. If you failed you were sent to a Secondary Modern School where rather than being only able to study in science and art you would be allocated to a basic English/Maths curriculum which would run alongside subjects like woodwork, metalwork, domestic science and art in preparation for getting a job in the adult world. In these schools you could leave at 15 to take up an apprenticeship, whereas, in the grammar school you were not allowed to leave before you were 16, when you would then elect to go out to find work in an office type environment or to stay on in the sixth form and study for 'A' levels with a view to applying and being accepted for university entrance. Both sets of students could also consider the possibility of moving on to further education in a technical college (mainly from age 12 onwards) where they could study for a national certificate in their chosen industry. After this they might go to a Polytechnic College.

I am not sure how long this whole system lasted but it did not seem long before the introduction of Comprehensive Schools. I think the main idea was to completely replace the secondary modern and grammar system with a single stream schooling system which would in itself be streamed. The lobby to keep grammar schools was strong and they have remained in many counties and continue to provide pre-university education. With the introduction of comprehensives the whole teaching pattern changed. In most cases purpose built schools were used and the idea that each child had his own desk where he/she could keep their belongings was thrown out and replaced with children carrying all their books from one class to another, where they went to the subject teacher instead of the teacher having his own class/form. These schools housed hundreds and sometimes even a thousand pupils. This created unforeseen logistical problems and did not make a quick start but it was never going to be allowed to fail. The new buildings were in general open plan and laid out to forms (Classes) but as mentioned although there was a desk space for each pupil, each pupil did not have a personal desk. This meant that instead of leaving text books pens and pencils etc. at a central point it was necessary to carry everything with you everywhere you went. What I saw was little kids carrying very heavy backpacks throughout the day, as well as to and from school. I thought we were creating the basis of an invalided teenage generation. I think I must have been wrong but I still wince when the young kids pass my window on the way to school. Could this burden be a reason these same youngsters do not appear to go out after school and play sport or do other energetic pass times.

Turning for a moment to a somewhat unrelated topic I will address the subject of school uniforms. First the lucky students who managed to get to a privileged school through examination success or by a local council or charity grant, it was often the case that the family could not afford to purchase the uniform. This meant that in some cases the local council were prepared to subsidise these purchases but much to the chagrin of the bright pupil they found all of their gear was tagged with the local council crest which singled them out from the other pupils. This was addressed in different ways by different families. The other end of the scale was no support and the family were left to get the best match utility clothing available on which they could embroider or stitch badges on as necessary; again not at all satisfactory. On the basic level a school uniform, in my opinion was one of the best things for schools and when it could be obtained at the school or a local shop at a reasonable price it made all pupils equal. When these rules were relaxed and kids could use designer trainers and own clothes, usually on Friday, this created an unhealthy atmosphere where items were stolen or children were bullied simply because not all families are equal. We all know this but do perhaps, unintentionally, promote the challenge of 'my families better than yours's'. Please return to school uniforms and leave the competition between the schools and not the individual pupils.

Where to go from here. There always seemed to be a faction about that felt that Universities were elitist and not really available to the lower classes. This was not true of the many kids that passed the 11 plus and made their way through academic achievement to a good university. The debate rumbled on but during the Thatcher Years she was not going to make changes to higher education because she had total belief in the grammar schools. Soon after John Major came to power the subject of the role of the polytechnic education became a hot topic. In 1992 all polytechnics were re-classed as fully fledged universities but in fact became regarded as 'new universities'. Whatever one's' thoughts were on this it was a done deal and the future was an anticipation that most students would move on to university and carve out a profitable career. It was then and has always been my belief that one cannot create equality and that the old order of meritocracy should and will prevail.

Alongside the changes to higher education in the early to mid-90s the primary education was also addressed and new exams called SATS were phased in. These, it would appear, were solely in order to track and monitor how well a school was performing. With the competition between universities to gain more entrants and parents to find the best school for their child the obvious unintended result was that the statistics became more important than anything else and the press and the quangos prepared an analysed the resultant ratings and the related created league tables. We had now come full circle and were running our education based on statistics. Guess what! These figures were not allowed to be looked at, at face value, but were first factored up or down to reflect all relevant impacts from location to social mix and background (how many single parent families and how many from two working parents etc.). The planning to take your children through this minefield was hard enough but then the government added a further dilemma. University fees! Having had all these university places made available they are now saying if you do not have funds then you have now lost the opportunity. No wait a minute you can still get all the benefits of this modern society as we will lend you the money to see you through to your degree. All you have to do is defer repayments and when you earn this new super wage you can repay from your monthly take home pay. In truth it could be that with all the graduates leaving university in their droves there will not be enough well paid jobs to go round. The high paid jobs become less well paid and we are back to the fifties where local universities were educating students to degree standard but there was not enough local work. They, as I have said before, took jobs in the local factories. Instead of the forecast sinecure we now have possible unemployment after graduation. I think our advisers forgot that there is also a law of supply and demand. There is also a distinct possibility that with the universities chasing new entrants each year the actual standard of the pass mark will reduce as they each look for a higher position in the league table. I have probably said too much but this comes from my being a bit old fashioned and believing in free access to both the NHS and a full education based, of course, on merit. I would not like to be up to £50,000 in debt before I have even got my first job.

CHAPTER NINETEEN

CONCLUSIONS

This whole first book has been my oversight of the political spectrum in the 1900s. I am hoping that you have benefited from my ramblings. I believe that in the course of writing this I have come to a number of conclusions with regard to the quality of government and its ability to govern.

I have decided that overall for many and varied reasons the government has gone astray, particularly in the second half of the century. Yes, they have become a nanny state as forecast in the book 'big brother is watching you'.

It is no accident that I mention two phrases which include common family titles. I feel that that government should be cut down to a more manageable size and have its responsibilities re-written in clear terms. It should be run as a father would run a good family environment without the interference of a nanny or brothers.

In a regular household there are three major concerns first making and keeping to a good set of rules, second managing within a budget and third looking after the health and family welfare.

I would like to take this analogy further and through to completing my summary and providing a dream of the future. The government is the father of the family, elected by his people to look after his flock. His main responsibility is to create a full set of rules and to ensure they are abided by. This means he needs a police force to manage crime and a court of law to impose relative punishment. Just one set of rules, one police force and one set of courts. No quangos electing themselves to be custodians and imposing fines through various unelected bodies. Proceed to step two and we need an NHS for health management but only for sickness accident and emergency backed up by good doctoring. As the child grows up and wants extra benefits they must be earned and therefore paid for. Welfare also means providing for the unfortunate members of the family who for some reason or another cannot provide for themselves. Dad tries to take care of this, but nobody is given hand outs before they have earnt them. Welfare also means teaching the offspring and this should be provided free up to when the kids are ready to leave the nest.

The third item is the budget. This is the amount the parent can earn to provide for his brood. The government can earn by profiting from the contracts it puts out to major projects, construction and possibly selling education as an export. By providing the environment and support for business, industry and commerce a natural outcome would be that these areas would self- finance and sensible taxation or specialist support could maintain a balanced economy. A good entrepreneur will find ways but this will need to be supplemented and as with my children when they started work I took one third of their wage packet to help the growing household costs. This becomes income tax. Most households take out insurance to cover emergencies and the government would be required to fund a regular armed service which as today would be managed by their own generals. There is certainly going to be a need to ensure that all parts of the jigsaw are performing as 'Fit for purpose' but this should be handled through the law and the one set of courts. Local councils should be treated like the children that fly the nest and bring up their own families. That is they build their own version of the family package. Unions, lobbying and charities will still be around but they would only have to work within the law and not have any direct input to government. Strikes would be illegal and arbitration would be legally enforced.

I think that this has covered all of the chapters that have gone before and with tongue in cheek I will now go forward to the technical and scientific innovations of the 1900s.

PART TWO

NATURAL PROGRESSION

CHAPTERS

CHAPTER ONE

CHURCHES

CONVENTIONAL RELIGION

Well here we go. I have just taken you through one of the three topics that should never be brought up in a discussion in a pub, politics! One of the other topics that is taboo in a pub is religion. I am entering this area but am not actually going to create a debate about the beliefs directly but rather to discuss the changes through religion that have had an impact during the1900s. In accordance with some of my previous topics I will start with a little history, and have decided to start with churches which generally came into being after heathen and progressive sects were prevalent prior to AD (anno domini). I will start on the assumption that modern religion started with Jesus Christ and has been supplemented by various sects and cults.

Christian Based Religions (Loosely). As at the start of the twentieth century the main churches, by which I mean the church as a body (religion?) not just a building, were Christian or bible related activities take place. I will detail a number of these with the occasional short added comment and then talk about the pseudo religious sect and cults that had significant impacts for a short period and in some cases are still active at the end of the century.

Existing religions at the beginning of the 1900s were mainly Christian or bible based and I will start with the one that goes back to the year AD. Other Christian church based religions will be added in approximate order of introduction to the U K.

Roman Catholic. Based on the bible and up until Henry the Eighth was the accepted universal practice for the majority of the nation. When Henry VIII wished to divorce and re-marry he fell out with the Pope and split from the Roman Holy See and declared himself head of the now newly formed Church of England.

The Church of England. This I understand was a replica of the Catholic Church but with variations at the behest of the King. He actually got very upset with the Catholics and throughout the Reformation he outlawed Catholicism and either destroyed the churches or converted them to the new Church of England denomination. This is simplistic but I feel sufficient for my discussion as it moves to the 20th century.

Church of Scotland. This governed by presbyteries - local bodies composed of minsters and elders – rather than by bishops, as was the case in England.

Ireland. Remained effectively Roman Catholic but in what became Northern Ireland the **Anglican** and **Scottish (Presbyterian)** churches had many adherents.

The **Puritan** movement gave rise to Nonconformist denominations, such as the **Baptists** and the **Congregationalists** that reflected the Puritan desire for simpler forms of worship and church government.

The Society of Friends (Quakers) also originated about this time. These were a Christian group believing in simplicity, equality and peace and dedicated to 'inward light' or direct apprehension of God, without creeds, clergy or other ecclesiastical forms.

Mid-18th century revivals gave Wales a form of Protestantism closely linked to the Welsh language the **Presbyterian Church of Wales** (or Calvinistic Methodism) which is still the most powerful religious body in the Principality.

Methodist. This is often most associated with John Wesley and spread particularly to Northumberland Durham and Yorkshire in the northeast and to Cornwall, which still has the largest percentage of Methodists.

The Salvation Army developed at this time when there was also an increase in the practice of **Judaism**. The **Jews** also settled in many of the large provincial cities but more than half of them lived in Greater London.

These church bodies were at the centre of everyday life and our laws seemed to somewhat replicate their generally high morals. This was reflected in the shops and industries having a working week that was made up of six working days and a day off (the Sabbath or Sunday). Bank holidays also incorporated religious festivals (Easter, Whitsun and Christmas). Taken to a different extreme the working man dressed up on Sunday's and went to church with his wife and then cleared off to the pup while she stayed home preparing the traditional roast lunch. Some men treated the pub as their church and failed to make the trip to the church. The kids often went to the church Sunday school, as mentioned earlier, often just to get a free outing, but also to get away from home. There were some kids who were likely to follow in their fathers' footsteps and spent many an hour sitting outside the pub hoping to be offered some pop and crisps. The elder children joined the boy's brigade and marched in their own band passed the church late on each Sunday morning and on high days and holidays. The Salvation Army came and played and prayed on street corners and handed out copies of their magazine War Cry and in the evening the Jehovah's came to the pubs and did likewise with Watch Tower and Awake!. During the week the church halls were the home to the teenage activities of Scouting, Guiding, Youth clubs and Army, Navy and Air Force Cadets.

These activities were all, in general, voluntary and run and supported by the ministers of the churches and local school teachers who were well respected and considered pillars of society (probably not always the case, but the system seemed to work).

This somewhat poor repetitive life existed virtually unchanged until the end of the Second World War, after which I think significant changes took place and these are what I will address next.

Historically the church was never directly involved in politics although the senior bishops were appointed to the House of Lords. These appointments were essentially to help the second chamber to provide a comprehensive review of what was passed to them from the House of Commons. With the increase in the number of liberal lobbying groups it was not long before the church were getting involved with the daily press and passing opinions on solely political issues. Many of these issues stemmed from the innovation within medicine and technology which I will address elsewhere. However I feel strongly that the church should have and still ought to stick to religion. As shown above each religion has a long history and in most cases a fully published book of rules (in most cases their interpretation of the bible). I do not believe that you should use the argument that life has changed and we need to adjust. Let the country and the politicians adjust but let the church carry on giving the fatherly guiding hand and maintain their proven principles.

My first recollections of clashes between religious and political liberals' opinions were in the late 40s and earlier 50s. This is a glib statement and is typical of the kind of remark I would make if I was asked for an opinion at short notice. Having thought about it I realise now that although I recognise the significant change in approach of the church to day-to-day non church activities I cannot and do not wish to list these individually as progressive specifics. As I said earlier I have already dealt with the general politics and I will now proceed to the evolution that I think has created these changes.

With the introduction of the computer age there was a dramatic increase in the speed of communications across the universe, and this, coupled with the improvement in general education, led to the younger generation becoming more aware of the scientific world around them. Blindly following their parents in both religion and politics was beginning to be challenged. This led to a significant reduction in regular churchgoers and therefore the church started to look more outward in the efforts to retain their congregations. I think that by the late 1900s the senior ministers of the church had started to forget that it was their religious beliefs that had taken them into the church and that it should be these beliefs that they needed to share. In truth change came gradually in relation to the speed of change outside of the church but the obvious feeling's that the changes in the way of life needed to be balanced were predominant. These progressed from the early challenges to traditions, particularly regarding family life, which could be considered specifically church related, to modern activities and moral translations, which often strayed well away from basic church beliefs.

Let me run through a number of these progressions in order for me to track this evolution. Soon after the war there was a high demand to rehome the children of war torn families and many charities became involved in this function. The new breed of liberal appeared and there was soon a heated debate as to whether churches should deal only with children of their own or whether all charities should handle all denominations, or none, equally. This was only a starter for similar differences to be exposed on no manner of changes that were available as a result of scientific, demographic and moral advances. In no particular order and definitely no bias these are some of the key subjects that had not been in most peoples' minds prior to the Second World War.

Contraception. There was already a difference of tolerance levels in the different churches which was divided between natural controls (self-control and rhythm etc.) and physical (the Dunlop Rubber Company i.e. condoms). Birth pills became available on the NHS prescriptions and coils and other less safe options were offered to women which meant that they had a much higher level of management over their future.

Single Mothers. Men apparently started to think it was no longer their responsibility to manage birth control but it was definitely not yet widespread for the women to manage it either. This resulted in more girls having an unwanted, but not necessarily unloved, child. This situation left the girl, at times, in the position where they were unwanted by both the careless male and also their parents. Obviously both the state and the church were very concerned about this and changes were implemented in the welfare system by the government.

Mixed Marriages. With influx of commonwealth citizens, from about the mid-fifties, a lot of our young girls took a fancy to the new breed of man available. Later when intercontinental travel became more readily available a number of eligible but not always young men visited the Far East and came back with a bride or a bride-to-be. Even later these young ladies started taking jobs in the U.K. and were found very attractive to the young men. These became mixed marriages and both the church and legal systems discussed the morals and the related adjustments that would be required, if any, to the relevant laws. The traditional British attitude was either to accept or decry these modern changes and in down to earth areas the attitude within and without the church was often to be anti and to suggest that they return to their own countries and stop stealing our youth. This gave rise to an early introduction of some local churches into political argument.

Working Women. With the modern world providing many goods at reasonable prices and the apparent ability of a young couple to obtain a mortgage; in the new more affluent society newly-weds started to be unwilling to start a new house with anything but new white goods and furniture. They in fact started to run before they could walk and found it a good idea for the new wife to wait, as was now a choice, to have a baby and to stay at work to fulfil their perceived requirements. With life being what it is, income and ambition changed, and holiday entitlement became longer each year; the perceived needs became greater and it became the norm for women, not only to work until the first baby came along, but to return to work as soon after as could be managed. Here again the church had very good moral, ethical and cannon law reasons to have their say in this matter but by now there was also a particular need for the state to provide proper welfare care for the resultant broken marriage outcomes bringing more single mothers and probably more uncared for children.

Divorce & Re-marrying. Although working mothers put stress onto the bliss of marriage there was also a new vibrant world that was calling to these young marrieds' but, unfortunately, both the husband and wife did not always find that with these changed opportunities, they actually agreed as well as they once had done. This simply added to the problems already described. The whole divorce process was also greatly modified around the 60s as up until then divorce was a very major event which was run through higher courts. I think that cruelty cases were always dealt with in one of the courts in the Inns in Fleet Street in the same way as bankruptcy where the poor soul had to leave through the back door into Carey

Street. It was a long drawn out, difficult and not cheap experience. Towards the end of the century it was so easy to arrange divorces that some people compared it to the quoted Arab equivalent where we are told the man only had to repeat three times 'I divorce you' and the marriage was decreed ended. In practice there are a whole army of lawyers earning lots of money advising each of the parties in order to facilitate a reasonable break with money, children and property properly accounted for.

Cremation. Having taken you through married life a new problem for the church came on the horizon in the form of a shortage of space in the existing graveyards. With the need for more housing close to the workplace land became a premium and local councils started to investigate the possibility of burning the dead and putting the ashes into a small cask for the family to do with what was the personal preference. Crematoriums evolved and were built with a garden of rest alongside. One could treat the garden of rest in the same way as an ordinary cemetery by having a small dedicated plaque displayed for perpetuity.

This appeared to go against the teachings of a number of religions but after all the debates about 'needs must', as the both options still remained, everyone was happy. In practice the lay people talked with their feet and chose the cremation route in the majority of cases. Where the churches see themselves today would appear to rest between the parishioner determining preferences (time, money and convenience) for themselves but the church retaining its' dogma for dedicated stalwarts. This is stronger in some religions than others and I cannot fully state differences for the likes of Jehovah Witnesses or Muslim and Hindu etc.

Church Unity. Throughout all of the above from around the mid-century all the Christian churches got together in an attempt to create complete or at least significant Unity. In fact the regular church goer did not see the reasoning and did not like the lip service, or dare I say politics that prevailed. The Catholics and Church of England reworded the last sentence of The Lord's Prayer and amended some of the order of service in the high services. The Catholic Church also notably changed from always using Latin and worldwide introduced local language to all regular Sunday services. Personally I found this particularly off-putting as I was working in Paris at the time, and where I could follow all of the service except for the sermon and the notices one week, the next week I felt like one of Christ's lost sheep. When I returned home I found that the local family service had been totally amended to take out the traditional hymns and Latin responses and replaced them with English and more modern unified hymns. This in my area saw a large loss of visitors for the Sunday Family Masses.

At this time I would say that church attendances dropped and it appeared that new sects were being investigated and immigration gave the impression that Muslim, Sikh and Hindu along with West Indian and Chinese were gaining ground and also that the Mormon and Jehovah Witnesses were to be found on your front door and in the local pubs promoting their cause.

Equal Rights/Human Rights. I am addressing this progression at this point as I cannot see me finding anywhere else to say my piece. I will try and stay to the way the church became involved and how at times they seemed to be trying to find an all-inclusive response instead of sticking to quoting their own beliefs and actions and allowing the world of dogooders and Health and Safety to get on in the real world. Why should I say this? Well the event that comes immediately to mind is the British Airways employee who claimed she was banned from wearing a crucifix. This was, of course, on the face of it, an honest opinion but it was deserving of proper analysis before the press and unions got involved. Apparently, not possible, but this was not the only time a possible Health and Safety or Employee uniform directive was deliberately ignored for political gain by some lobby group or another. The problem I have here is why, just because it was a crucifix, the church had to get involved. In my own experience I had to ensure that staff working with certain machinery had to take special precautions which meant that men and women were banned from wearing flapping necklaces. I did not check whether any of these had holy/religious accoutrements as this ban was a necessity. We did not have any uprising or union objections. This shows how things can be done but I would certainly not have welcomed the person's local minister calling me to complain or even think it appropriate. Church putting their oar in unnecessarily alienates them from their real vocation and I feel this is another reason that attendances were steadily reducing. I joined Equal Rights to this as I did not want to repeat my argument which also applies to equal opportunity, particular examples are equal pay and fat cat directors, why when they cannot achieve church Unity should they try and get involved in non-religious matters.

Miscellany. Political actions that do not fit directly into a specific category but are worth consideration are firstly, **The Common Market** which started in around the early 60s, when the government started negotiations with Europe, apparently based solely on trade, but which as we know morphed through several transitions into the **European Union,** had the church heavily involved. I do not think this did anything to further the spread of the faith within the country. Secondly the church hierarchy, in response to perceived vandalism, advised that all local churches consider keeping their **doors locked** except for services and at other special occasions. Was this the way to attract a new and larger congregation? No! It alienated the casual visitor who was interested in the building or discovering what went on inside. They also seemed to think that their cathedrals were so prestigious that they should earn income by charging for entry. Fine for the devoted tourist but again what about the casual visitor and the traveller looking for a place of solace for private prayer. The next thing that moved people away from the churches was the change in the law which allowed private manors, castles and country residences, later to include hotels, to provide **complete wedding packages** which could include the wedding prelims, the wedding, the reception dinner and the late night disco. This is probably not comprehensive but covers the ground and brings me to the last big event of the 1900s.

Brexit. Britain leaving the European Union. This is all to do with business and the economy but right through the process the Archbishop of Canterbury's statements have been regularly released to the press. Unnecessary and unproductive. It is no wonder that some of our youth and celebrities have turned to exploring alternatives to Christianity and bible related religion.

Cults and Sects

Having said that the church was changing and science was, in the young peoples' minds, challenging how it was possible to believe in the mysteries propounded by most religions. It was not only science that they found interesting but also the fringe, maybe pseudo, sects and cults. This from my memory began with Flower Power in San Francisco and the Beatles with their involvement in Transcendental Meditation. I will now describe some of these in some detail but will not be able to either name or explain the rest of well over 100 groups that came, went or remain now.

Christian group. I found this in a website: <u>the aims of the group</u>. They were Simplicity, Equality and Peace, and they were dedicated to 'Inward Light' or Direct Apprehension of God, without Creeds, Clergy or other Ecclesiastical Forms. I wrote this down at the time and wondered who these people were and how I should, if I felt the need, contact them. My only reaction was maybe there was somewhere a direct line to God. I am sorry but I do not naturally understand fringe activities but that aside I will continue. (This quote came, I think, from the early Quakers as mentioned above).

Flower Power. This term originated in the mid-60s in the wake of a film version of H. G. Wells book 'The Time Machine' that depicted flower-bestowing, communal people of the future, in a story characterised by anti-war themes. Political Activists advocated the giving of flowers as a means of peaceful protest. Flower Power popularised the association of flowers with the counterculture movement of the1970s. Particularly the Hippies who embraced the symbolism by dressing in clothing with embroidered flowers and vibrant colours, wearing flowers in their hair and distributing flowers to the public, becoming known as flower children. In 1967 100,000 young people from all over the world flocked to San Francisco to 'wear some flowers in their hair'. The festival's billing was music, love and flowers. Not exactly a fully formalised sect or a cult I feel but definitely an early indication of change.

Transcendental Meditation. This was more of a technique like yoga which had started out around 1939. Maharishi Mahesh Yogi became a disciple and was the spiritual leader of the Indian City of Jyotir Math. He began the Spiritual Regeneration Movement in 1957 in Madras, India, and the following year took his techniques worldwide. The Beatles had encountered Maharishi as kids up north and they say he appeared on telly every few years. They met him in 1967 and visited him in India in 1968. Where is this today?

Osho. (Bhagwan Shree Rajneesh) introduced the practice of 'dynamic meditation and became a spiritual teacher and began to attract a significant following. Concurrent with his teaching at University of Jabalpur, Rajneesh travelled throughout India, spreading his unconventional and controversial ideas about spirituality. Among his teachings was the notion that sex was the first step toward achieving 'superconsciousness'. By 1964 he started conducting meditation camps and recruiting followers, and two years later he resigned from his professorship to focus more fully on spreading his spiritual teachings. In the process he became something of a pariah and earned himself the nickname 'the sex guru'.

The 1970 he introduced the practice of 'dynamic meditation' which he asserted, enables people to experience divinity. The prospect enticed young westerners to come and reside at his ashram in Pune, India, and become devout disciples called sannyasins. In their quest for spiritual enlightenment these followers took new Indian names, dressed in orange and red clothes, and participated in group sessions that sometimes involved violence and sexual promiscuity. By the late 70s, the six-acre ashram was so overcrowded that Rajneesh sought a new site to relocate to. However his movement had become so controversial that the local government threw up various roadblocks to make things difficult for him. Tensions came to a head in 1980, when a Hindu fundamentalist attempted to assassinate him.

Facing ongoing pressure from government authorities and traditional religious groups, in 1981 he fled to the United States with 2000 of his followers, settling on a 100 square mile ranch in central Oregon. Here they started to build their own city. Disapproving neighbours contacted local officials in an attempt to close him down but he won the court case and continued to expand the commune.

As tensions between the commune and the local government community increased, he and his followers soon turned to more drastic measures to achieve their ends, including murder, wiretapping, voter fraud, arson and a mass salmonella poisoning in 1984 affecting more than 700 people.

After several of his leaders left to avoid prosecution, in 1985 Rajneesh was arrested. Charged with immigration fraud he arranged a plea bargain and returned to India, where he found that the number of his followers had decreased significantly.

He then searched unsuccessfully for a place to re-establish his ashram. He was denied entry into numerous countries before returning again to India in 1986. During the coming years he continued to teach and renamed himself Osho, but his health began to decline and he died in October 1990 at one of his few remaining communes in Pune, India. Following his death, the commune was renamed the Osho Institute, and then later the Osho International Meditation Resort, which is currently estimated to attract as many as 200,000 visitors a year. Osho followers also continue to spread his belief from one of the hundreds of Osho Meditation Centers that they have opened in major cities across the globe.

I am including these cults with apparently abhorrent practices to ensure I complete a picture. You will notice this in quite a number in the coming groups and I will not comment further on the spiritual benefits either in a positive or a negative sense.

Scientology is a body of religious beliefs and practices first described in 1950 and organised as a movement in May 1952 by American author L Ron Hubbard. He initially developed a program of ideas called Dianetics which was distributed through the Dianetics Foundation. The foundation soon entered bankruptcy and Hubbard lost the rights to his seminal publication in 1952. He then re-characterised the subject as a religion and renamed it Scientology.

L Ron Hubbard was an only child born in America in 1911. In 1938 he reportedly reacted to a drug used in a dental procedure. According to his account, this triggered a revelatory near-death experience. He wrote or co-wrote an unpublished book with a working title 'The One Command' which revisited Dianetics , the set of ideas and practices regarding the metaphysical relationship between the mind and body which became the central philosophy of Scientology. Hubbard was commissioned in the American Forces in 1943. He reported stomach pains in April 1945 and spent the rest of the war in a naval hospital. According to his later teachings, during this time he made scientific 'breakthroughs' by the use of 'endoctrine experiments'. In October 1947 he requested psychiatric treatment, which he could not afford, from the Veterans Administration. Within a few years he would condemn psychiatry as evil, and this would grow into a major theme in Scientology.

1950 saw the publication of Hubbard's Dianetics: The Evolution of a Science. In the same year he published a book Dianetics: The Modern Science of Mental Health, considered the seminal event of the century by Scientologists who sometimes use a dating system based on the book's publication; for example, 'A.D.28' which does not stand for Anno Domini, but 'After Dianetics'. **Dianetics** uses a counselling technique known as auditing in which an auditor assists a subject in conscious recall of traumatic events in the individuals past. It was originally intended to be a new psychotherapy and was not expected to become the foundation of a new religion.

In April 1953 Hubbard wrote a letter proposing that Scientology should be transformed into a religion. As membership declined and money grew tighter, Hubbard had reversed the hostility to religion he had voiced in Dianetics. His letter discussed the legal and financial benefits of religious status. He outlined plans for setting up a chain of 'Spiritual Guidance Centers' charging customers $500 for 24 hours auditing ('that's real money...... Charge enough and we'd be swamped') he wrote.

In December 1953, Hubbard incorporated three churches – a 'Church of American Science', a 'Church of Scientology' and a 'Church of Spiritual Engineering' – in Camden, New Jersey.

In 1954, with his blessing, some of his followers set up the first Church of Scientology, the Church of Scientology of California, adopting the 'aims, purposes, principles and creed of the Church of American Science, as founded by L Ron Hubbard'. The movement moved quickly through the United States and to other English-speaking countries. The second Church of Scientology to be set up after the one in California, was in Auckland, New Zealand. England had a British headquarters in Saint Hill Manor, Saint Hill Green, East Grinstead in Kent. In 1955 he established the Founding Church of Scientology in Washington D C. The Church experienced further challenges. The U S Food and drug Administration investigated E-Meters claiming they were illegal medical devices. Eventually the Court ordered the Church to label every meter with a disclaimer that it is purely a religious artefact. In the course of developing Scientology, Hubbard presented rapidly changing teachings that some have described as self-contradictory.

In 1966 Hubbard purportedly stepped down as executive director of Scientology to devote himself to research and writing.

In 1972, facing criminal charges in France, Hubbard returned to the United States and began living in an apartment in New York. When faced with possible indictment in the U S, he went into hiding in April 1979. Later in 1979 the FBI raided the Church Guardian's Office and arrested and convicted eleven senior people of obstructing justice, burglary of government offices, and theft of documents and government property. In 1981 Scientology took the German government to court for the first time. On January 24th, 1986 L Ron Hubbard died.

I can only complete this narrative by quoting the man himself when he described Scientology as an 'applied religious philosophy' because, according to him, it consists of 'a metaphysical doctrine, a theory of psychology, and teachings in morality'. The core of Scientology lies in the belief that 'each human has a reactive mind that responds to life's traumas, clouding the analytic mind and keeping us from experiencing reality'. I should also state that a number of A-List celebrities have been active members of this religion.

Unification Church, byname of **Holy Spirit Association for the Unification of World Christianity**, religious movement founded in Pusan, South Korea, by the Reverend Sun Myung Moon in 1954. It became known for its mass weddings, I seem to remember some were in lakes, and its members were commonly referred to as **'Moonies'**. The church taught a unique Christian theology.

Born in 1920 moon was brought in the Presbyterian Church, which eventually excommunicated him for heresy. As a teenager he had a vision in which he was charged with completing Jesus' unfinished work. Accepting this call, he began to preach, faced persecution from the government, and founded the church.

Moon preached that the world was created from God's inner nature, which reflected in the 'dual' expressions of life, Sung Sang (casual, masculine) and Hyung Sang (resultant, feminine). The purpose of creation, moon said, was to experience the joy of love. Adam and Eve, however, sinned by misusing love and failed to realise God's purpose. In the wake of their failure, selfish love has dominated human existence, and God has sought to restore his original plan. God's efforts at 'restoration', which require the intervention of the Messiah, have been continually thwarted. Although Jesus was able to create the conditions necessary for humanity's spiritual salvation, he did not marry and thus, did not complete God's plan.

The Unification Church identifies Moon as the Messiah who will implant God's heart of love into his followers and complete Jesus' works. Having married and raised the 'ideal' family, moon called on members of the church to follow his example and thereby participate in God's plan for restoration. God's kingdom on Earth would be established by his followers accepting the blessing of their marriage in one of his mass wedding ceremonies for which his church became known.

In the late 1950s the church spread to the West and in the 70s was identified as a 'cult'. Parents protested that their children's membership in the group often damaged careers and family ties. They sought the help of deprogrammers and filed civil lawsuits. Controversy surrounding the church led to congressional hearings and in 1982 Moon was convicted of tax evasion. Supporters and other church leaders felt this was an example of government religious persecutions.

Having gone through a period of severe criticism, the Unification Church emerged in the 1990s with an expansive international program. The church has a presence in over 100 countries although true membership figures are not definitive. Its influence is extended by a variety of organisations that embody Moon's ideals, such as the Professor's World peace Academy and the International Conference on the Unity of Sciences. On its 40th anniversary in 1994 Moon announced the formation of the International Federation for World Peace, which assumed many of the functions formerly performed by the church.

Although the early 1990s was a period of relative stability for the Unification movement, problems arose for the church in Japan following the AUM Shinrikyo incident in1995, when the country was gripped by anticult hysteria. The church was also hurt when Moon's daughter-in-law, Nansook Hong, in 1998 wrote an expose of life in the Moon family.

Jehovah's Witnesses is a millenarian restorationist Christian denomination with nontrinitarian beliefs distinct from mainstream Christianity. The group reports worldwide membership over 8 million involved in evangelism and an annual Memorial attendance of 20 million. They believe that the destruction of the present world system at Armageddon is imminent, and that the establishment of God's kingdom over the earth is the only solution for all problems faced by humanity.

The group emerged from the Bible Student movement founded in the late 1870s by Charles Taze Russell who was president of the Watch Tower Society when he died in October 1916. In 1917 Joseph Franklin Rutherford was elected as its next president.

In July 1931, at a convention in Columbus, Ohio, Rutherford introduced the new name – Jehovah's Witnesses – based on Isaiah 43:10 as written in the New World Translation of the Holy Scriptures (their own bible) – which was adopted by resolution. The name was chosen to distinguish his group of Bible Students from other independent groups that had severed ties with the Society, as well as symbolise the instigation of new outlooks and the promotion of fresh evangelising methods.

Jehovah's Witnesses are best known for their door-to-door preaching, distributing literature such as Watchtower and Awake! and for refusing military service and blood transfusions. They consider the use of God's name vital for proper worship. They reject Trinitarianism, inherent immortality of the soul and hellfire, which they consider to be unscriptural doctrines. They do not observe Christmas, Easter, birthdays or other holidays and customs they consider to have pagan origins incompatible with Christianity.

The group's position regarding conscientious objection to military service and refusal to salute state symbols (like national anthems and flags) has brought it into conflict with some governments. This has at times led to mob violence and further government opposition in major countries like the United States, Canada, Germany and more. Consequently some Jehovah's Witnesses have been persecuted and their activities are banned or restricted in some countries. However, their challenges have influenced legislation related to civil rights in several countries.

Nathan Knorr was appointed the third president of the Watch Tower Bible and Tract Society in 1942 and commissioned a new translation of the Bible: New World translation of the Holy Scriptures, the full version of which was released in1961.

From 1966, Witness publications and convention talks built anticipation of the possibility that Christ's thousand-year reign might begin in late 1975 or shortly thereafter. By 1975 the active membership exceeded 2 million. Membership declined during the late 1970s after expectations for 1975 were proved wrong. Watch Tower literature did not state dogmatically that 1975 would definitely mark the end, but in 1980 the Watch Tower society admitted its responsibility in building hope regarding that year.

My personal experience of this religion was that it felt like they brainwashed their members and then were able to dictate to them. This resulted in a number of family and friends being kept apart from each other in promotional and weekly meetings. The youngsters were given tasks each week to study the Bible and prepare presentations based on picking out several words from the book and relating them to each other rather than looking at them in context. This appeared to be preparing them for their doorstep visits.

This is still one of the strongest of religions to be developed through the 1900s.

The foregoing sects/cults from Flower power onward have all been reasonably reputable organisations. The following six cults are examples where 'spiritual' groups are perceived to have 'gone too far'. You will understand this after my further resumes.

The Manson Family Cult was headed by Charles Manson who organised a murderous campaign that would make him one of the most infamous figures in criminal history.

'The Family' was a group of around 100 followers of Manson who shared his passion for an unconventional lifestyle and habitual use of hallucinogenic drugs, such as LSD and magic mushrooms. The Family moved from San Francisco to a deserted ranch in San Fernando Valley. Manson's followers also included a small, hard-core unit of impressionable young girls. They began to believe, without question, Manson's claims that he was Jesus and his prophecies of race war. Manson was influenced by The Beatles song 'Helter Skelter' which he interpreted as incitation to begin a race war. He turned to the 1968 album and lyrics to justify his scheme and to guide his followers to murder.

Manson had a strong belief and interest in the notion of Armageddon from the book of revelations, and also explored the teachings of Scientology and more obscure cult churches, such as the Church of Final Judgement. In many ways, Manson reflected personality traits and obsessions for gurus of cult-quasi-religious groups that began to emerge in the 1960s. He was pathologically deluded into believing that he was the harbinger of doom regarding the planet's future.

Notorious for his connection to the brutal slayings of the pregnant actress Sharon Tate and other Hollywood residents. He received the death penalty in 1971, a sentence that was commuted to life in prison the following year.

The Branch Davidians. Although this extremist branch sect of the Seventh Day Adventists has been active since the 1950s the Branch Davidians are better known for their activities after David Koresh, brought up as a Seventh Day Adventist by his grandparents, joined them in in the early 1980s. Then known as Vernon Powell he had an affair with the sect's much older prophetess, Lois Roden, and in 1984, he married a teenaged Branch Davidian named Rachel Jones, with whom he had two children.

When Roden passed away, Koresh and Roden's son, George argued over who would take over the Branch Davidians. Koresh left the sect with his followers and lived in eastern Texas for a while. In 1987 he and a handful of devotees returned to Mount Carmel heavily armed and shot George

Roden, who survived the attack. Koresh and his crew were tried for attempted murder but were acquitted.

In 1990, he legally changed his name from Howell to Koresh (after the Persian king) and became the Branch Davidians' leader. Koresh's teachings included the practice of 'spiritual weddings' which enabled him to bed God-chosen female followers of all ages. He fathered at least a dozen children with members other than his legal wife. The group believed the apocalypse was imminent and, fearing its arrival, locked themselves into a sprawling compound. They built an 'Army of God' by stockpiling weapons in preparation for the apocalypse. On 28th February 1993, the Federal Bureau of Alcohol, Tobacco and Firearms raided the Davidians compound outside of Waco, Texas, resulting in a 51 day siege that drew national attention. The standoff ended when the compound erupted in flames on April 19th: Koresh, who shot himself, was among the around 80 people found dead.

Peoples Temple began as a church in the Pentecostal-Holiness tradition in Indianapolis in the 1950s. In a deeply segregated city, it was one of the few places where black and white working-class congregants sat together in church on a Sunday Morning. Its members provided various kinds of assistance to the poor – food, clothing, housing, legal advice – and the church and its pastor, Jim Jones, gained a reputation for fostering racial integration. The income generated through licensed care homes, operated by Jim Jones' wife, Marceline, subsidised The Free Restaurant, a cafeteria where anyone could eat at no cost. Church members also mobilised to promote desegregation efforts at local restaurants and businesses, and the Temple formed an employment service that placed African-Americans in a number of entry level positions. While this has since become an active part of many churches since, at that time it was, innovative, even radical, for the 1950s.

In the mid-1960s, more than 80 members of the group packed up and headed west together.

Under the guidance of Marceline, the Temple acquired a number of properties in the Redwood Valley and established nine residential care facilities for the elderly, six homes for foster children, and Happy Acres, a state-licensed ranch for mentally- disabled adults. In addition, Temple families took in others needing assistance through informal networks.

The Temple expanded south to San Francisco, and eventually to Los Angeles.

Jim Jones was a committed communist and he wanted to demonstrate Marxism through his church.

In order to increase publicity, the Peoples Temple organised large religious 'conventions' with other Pentecostal pastors, with Jones continuing to disguise the fact that he was using religion to further his political ideology.

In 1974 the Peoples Temple signed a lease to rent land in Guyana. The community created on this property was called the Peoples Temple Agricultural Project or, informally, 'Jonestown'. It had under 100 members in early 1977.

Jones saw Jonestown as both a 'socialist paradise' and a 'sanctuary' from media scrutiny. Jones who was the self-proclaimed 'messiah' of his evangelical flock led them to Jonestown which he described as an agricultural commune rich with food, where there were no mosquitoes or snakes and where temperatures hovered around a perfect 72 degrees every single day.

In truth some people described the project as a prison camp. And in several ways this was true as people were not free to leave and dissidents were cruelly punished. Others have apparently described it as heaven on earth. But then there is the final day.

On November 17th, 1978 a U S Congressman from San Francisco area investigating claims of abuse within the Peoples Temple, visited Jonestown. During the visit a number of the Temple members expressed a desire to leave with him and on November 18th they accompanied him to the local airstrip at Port Kaituma. There they were intercepted by self – styled Temple security guards who opened fire on the group, killing the Congressman, three journalists, and one of the defectors. A few seconds of gunfire from the incident were captured on video by one of the journalists killed in the attack.

That evening, in Jonestown, Jones ordered his congregation to drink a concoction of cyanide-laced, grape-flavoured Flavor Aid. In all 912 people died including 276 children. This mass drinking of the Flavor Aid had sadly been carefully rehearsed on a number of occasions.

According to the press Jones died of a gunshot wound to the head. At that time it was the greatest single loss of American civilian life in a deliberate act. Needless to say the Temple was unable to continue in other areas.

The Sullivanians. Saul B Newton founded The Sullivan Institute in 1957 with his wife, Dr. Jane Pearce, in an attempt to create a viable alternative to the traditional nuclear family, which he viewed as the root of all social anxiety. The Sullivan Institute operated as both a therapy center and a polyamorous commune, despite the fact that Newton, the leader, had no formal training as a therapist. Unlike other practicing therapists who worked under a strict code of ethics, there were no such boundaries for the Sullivanians, as members of the Institute were known, with therapists and other members of the community sleeping with each other regularly. In fact, they were forbidden from engaging in exclusive relationships. Any children born to Sullivanians were sent away to boarding school or caretakers with very little visitation from their parents. All members were encouraged to cut ties with their former friends and family members. In the 1970s, the group, which had about 500 members, merged with a progressive theatre collective called the Fourth Wall and relocated to Orlando in 1979 following the nuclear meltdown at Three Mile Island. After seeing a decline in membership in the 1980s the Sullivanians ended with the death of Newton in 1991.

Children of God. David 'Moses' Borg founded this communist Christian offshoot in California in 1968. For someone so concerned with moral decay and evolution, Borg had a very sex-centric perspective on how to spread the views of Jesus, including reported recruitment through 'flirty fishing' (using young women to lure new members by having sex with them) and apparently opposing anti-paedophilia laws. According to some former members, having sex with children was not only permitted, but was also a divine right. Berg was a master of propaganda and published and distributed pamphlets discussing his teachings. The group still exists in 80 countries, including in Bromley, Kent, England, although no longer permits sex between adults and children. Here again known actors have joined and left this cult.

Heaven's Gate founded in 1972 by Marshall Applewhite and Bonnie Nettles, was based on the promise, that aliens would escort members of the group to the 'Kingdom of Heaven' via extra-terrestrial spacecraft. They first made headlines in 1975, when they convinced 20 new followers to give up their earthly possessions, leave their families and disappear. On the news it was described as a mystery whether they had been taken or were on a so-called trip to eternity, perhaps simply taken. (They turned out to be living underground, camping everywhere from Rhode Island to Oklahoma).

Heaven's Gate is best known for a much more tragic event two decades later. In March 1997 the group carefully planned and then executed a mass suicide, timed to coincide with the arrival of the Hale-Bopp comet, which members thought would conceal the alien spacecraft on its way to earth. Clad in black tunics and Nikes, 39 Heaven's gate members ate apple sauce mix chased with a sedative and vodka, covered their heads in plastic bags and died. Nine of the men, including Applewhite, Had been surgically castrated, as the group mandated celibacy. An upbeat videotaped message made by the members prior to the suicide indicated that they were willing, even happy, to die and move to the 'next level'. This cult also died with its founder.

Well, that is it. That is what you might think. Well it is the end of what I am going to say with regards to the additions and changes to the church in the 1900s. I now ask myself the question, what can I take from this?

I have found it informative but it does not show any truly revelatory changes either to the church or as a result of attempts of the sects and cults to introduce new visions.

It has however shown significant changes to, how the churches go about their job, and how the everyday man/woman has proceeded in this respect. I feel, as I have mentioned before that the church could learn from this analysis and return to more traditional missionary work without the historical coercion and some bloodshed. The ability of the fringe cults to recruit such large followings and exposure tells me that, the young in particular, are a little disenchanted with the current offerings and are willing to experiment. In the coming chapters I will track many real innovative progressions which have been truly awesome in their time. The development has been so vast and so quick that it may be a reason why the old slow ways are being challenged. This is right for most instances but with the church it does not seem appropriate to move the goalposts.

CHAPTER TWO

SCIENCE

I have decided that this should be introduced now as a precursor to the innovations that have been developed in the 1900s. The major advances in the 1900s come in medicine, communications and travel in the broadest sense, which have all evolved from the three basic sciences, Physics, Chemistry and Biology.

Going back to when I was at school my history for GCE was based on the ancient ages of stone, iron, and bronze etc. which took me back to the original early inventions like tools, wheels, fire and rope to name but a few. By the beginning of the 1900s, which is my chosen subject, we already had, water power, steam power engines, and internal combustion engines along with gas and a little electricity. All of these were to become the inspirations for the amazing changes to be brought in during the 20th century. The speed of these changes could not have been imagined if you were a youngster at the beginning of the 1900s but my next chapters will try and describe and put into perspective this progress which I feel is better addressed initially under the three main headings of Medical, Transport and Technology followed by several expansions, and then a chapter on Life and a conclusion.

CHAPTER 3

MEDICAL

This is interesting as we know that many physicians have been renowned over the centuries but the rate of change especially from the 1930s onwards was so dramatic that I will only attempt to list all of the marvellous improvements with a short note or appropriate comment.

Vaccinations/Inoculations.

Smallpox and vaccination are intimately connected. Edward Jenner developed the first vaccine to prevent smallpox infections in 1796, and this success led to the global eradication of smallpox and the development of many life-saving vaccines.

The smallpox vaccination is based on a thousand year old technique called inoculation, in which a small sample of infected matter is deliberately introduced to the body in order to prevent the full disease from developing. Today people can get vaccines against a whole host of infectious diseases, but smallpox is not one of them. Thanks to the global eradication programme of mass vaccination, the entire world population was officially free from this life-threatening disease by 1979.

In the late 1940s vaccines were recommended for:

Smallpox

Diphtheria

Tetanus

Pertussis (Whooping Cough)

Polio was an horrendous problem and when in 1955 a vaccine was licensed, John Salk, its inventor, became an overnight hero.

Measles

Mumps

Rubella (German Measles)

Were all added in the 60s and in the 1980s Hepatitis B and Haemophilus influenza type b were further licensed. Later in the century varicella (chickenpox 1996), rotavirus (a disease which affects nearly every child in the world under five, 1998) and hepatitis A (2000) became available.

This has almost all been positive proof of the effectiveness of vaccines and the travel inoculations for malaria, yellow fever etc. have shown a high level of success. But let us now consider the 'flu jab'. This is intended to protect many hundreds of thousands and reduce the sometimes many thousands of deaths each year. Unfortunately flu is a virus and has numerous variants and as the vaccine has to be made at least a year in advance it becomes somewhat of a guessing game as to which variant is coming next. The end result has been that some years the vaccine has been virtually ineffective. I do not think this should be regarded as a failing but for the public to be made fully aware of the problems and recognise that viruses are not like diseases that could in the long run be eliminated.

Limb and Joint Replacement.

This has been seen as a nice to have for most of time, in fact, some years ago a 3000-year old mummy was unearthed and revealed the presence of a wooden prosthetic toe. This was equipped with straps to attach to the foot and leg, while the toe was even made to flex, amazing for that period. Thanks to extraordinary advancements in technology, the development, and design of prosthetics have greatly improved.

Going back to the middle ages, many times if a person lost a hand or a leg they would be fitted with a wooden 'peg leg' or 'hook hand' as they came to be known. However it was not until after world war two that more sophisticated limbs made from a combination of leather and wood became common. Between the 1970s and 1990s more significant advancements in prosthetics were achieved and developers introduced the use of plastics, polycarbonates, resins and laminates to the world, allowing for a lighter and manageable design. Additionally, synthetic sockets were created in order to provide patients with tailored comfort.

As at the end of the century the situation with regard to whole or partial limb replacement was not changed as to reason or execution but the limb itself was considerably more useful and looked like it would soon get even better. The equivalent to the ropes, pulleys and springs, hopefully, would be replaced with electronics.

The development of sockets meant that operations for replacement joints was now possible and in fact these were one of the most successful innovations in surgery in that from the very first operation they proved a resounding hit with early versions lasting ten to fifteen years. This was to gradually increase to about 25years.

Most need for replacement surgery was to relieve the pain of osteoarthritis and I will list the current available surgery based on the numbers of operations and the quality of the results.

Hip Replacement. This is by far the most frequent and nowadays the least painful and long lasting. The first total joint replacement (also known as arthroplasty) was developed by John Charnley, a doctor and researcher in England. His first replacement hip in 1960 consisted of a metal stem with a plastic cap, affixed to the person's real bones with cement and an orthopaedic surgeon in America said, 'This device was immediately highly successful', the benefits of a good result is very rewarding 'by that I mean it relieved pain and allowed people to get back to their daily routines'

Knee Replacements. These were not initially effective, but now their success rates have almost caught up with artificial hips. The old way of gluing bones did not really work on the heavier individual and after about 30 years of trying they discovered a technique that makes cement obsolete: bone can attach itself to a rough metal surface by growing into it, much like bone heals after a fracture.

Foot and Ankle

Hand and Wrist

Shoulder and Elbow

All three of these ops are at a fairly early stage and only recommended in extreme cases.

Organ Replacement.

The amazing thing about organ transplants is the progress made during the second half of the 20th century. The first heart transplant by the South African, Christian Barnard in 1967 was the first organ replacement that I had heard of in my lifetime. Now organs and tissues that can be transplanted include:

Liver

Kidney

Pancreas

Heart

Lung

Intestine

Cornea

Middle ear

Skin

Bone Marrow

Heart valves

Vascularised composite allografts (transplant of several structures that may include skin, bone, muscles, blood vessels, nerves, and connective tissue).

A lot of these are rare or not popularly known so I will now give a little background and or comment on the major impact ones that we encounter regularly in conversation and, almost without thinking take it for granted that these are simple processes. No operation is without possible serious outcomes either before, during or after the operation itself, anaesthetics, blood loss or later infection, are but a few concerns.

Heart. From 1938, after the first operation on the heart vessels to repair a pulmonary artery defect was successful progress has been steady and in the 1950s a major step forward was when surgeons experimented with lowering the patient's body temperature which allowed the first successful open heart surgery in 1952. The heart-lung machine was then developed, this takes over the functions of the body's vital organs, giving the surgeon more time to operate. Then after the 1967 transplant this procedure became so successful and wide spread that during the1970s there was a shortage of donor hearts.

Surgeons had been experimenting with artificial heart transplants since the 1950s, but it was not until nearly the end of the century, that battery powered heart transplants proved successful. The artificial hearts give the patient time to recover or wait for a donor heart to be found. It was hoped that these might then soon become long term solutions to heart defects.

1983 - The first combined heart and lung transplant is performed by Sir Magdi Yacoub at Harefield Hospital.

Liver. The first truly successful liver transplant was performed in 1967. 1965 - A kidney transplant in the UK uses an organ donated from a dead person for the first time. 1967 - The world's first heart transplant was performed in South Africa by Dr Christian Barnard. Louis Washkansky received the heart of a young woman. Liver transplants became available nationally in 1983.

You would normally require a liver transplant as a result of severe damage through, cirrhosis, hepatitis or metabolic conditions inside the liver.

Kidney. 1954 - The first successful kidney transplant operation is performed by Dr Joseph Murray in Boston, Massachusetts. The technique has since saved hundreds of thousands of lives worldwide, and many thousands of kidney transplants are now carried out in the UK each year.

Cornea. 1983 - Launch of the Corneal Transplant Service with support from the Iris Fund for the prevention of blindness. Corneal transplants now save the sight of some 2000 plus patients in the UK every year.

1986 - The Bristol Eye Bank is established as part of the Corneal Transplant Service's national network. Donated corneas can be stored for up to four weeks before transplant and the Bristol Centre sends some 1,500 corneas around the country for transplant surgery.

1989 - The Manchester Eye Bank opens at Manchester Royal Hospital.

Pancreas Transplants The University of Minnesota performed the first-ever pancreas transplant, in December 1966 it was undertaken at the University of Minnesota by surgeons Richard Lillehei and William Kelly.

A pancreas transplant can restore normal insulin production and improve blood sugar control in people with diabetes, but it's not a standard treatment. The side effects of the anti-rejection medications required after a pancreas transplant can often be serious.

My wife, an insulin dependent for more than 25 years tells me she would rather carry on the personal control regime than have the worry and risk of a transplant.

Lung Transplants. Dr. James Hardy performed the first human lung transplant in 1963 in Jackson Mississippi. Before proceeding with human lung transplantation, Dr. Hardy and his team had performed approximately 400 transplant experiments on dogs

The first clinical attempt in humans was reported by Hardy and Webb in 1963 followed by others with short survival only except for one case by Derom *et al.* who lived for 10 months. Long-term successes were not reported until after the discovery of cyclosporine as a new immunosuppressive agent. Successful heart-lung transplantation (HLTx) for pulmonary vascular disease was performed by the Stanford group starting in 1981 while the Toronto group described good outcome after single-lung transplantation (SLTx) for pulmonary fibrosis in 1983 and after double-lung transplantation for emphysema in 1986. The evolution in lung transplantation still continued with the use of pulmonary allografts coming from living-related donors, from donors after circulatory death, or after prior assessment and reconditioning during ex vivo lung perfusion (EVLP) in an attempt to overcome the critical shortage of suitable organs. Early outcome has significantly improved over the last three decades. Better treatment and prevention of chronic lung allograft dysfunction will hopefully result in further improvement of long-term survival after lung transplantation

The third HLTx (heart-lung transplant) was performed in July, 1971 in Cape Town, South Africa by Christian Barnard who seems to be a lead figure in most of my transplant surveys.

The first long-term success of human heart-lung transplantation was performed by Bruce Reitz and colleagues at Stanford University, Palo Alto, California, on March 9, 1981. This patient survived, thanks to the improved surgical technique and the use of cyclosporine. The patient was a 45-year old woman with primary pulmonary hypertension (PPH). She suffered two acute rejection episodes successfully reversed, with a good lung function preserved for a long time. Two more patients underwent the same operation during the following 4 months.

In 1983, a 58-year-old patient with IPF with the above mentioned characteristics inquired for the possibility of a transplant in Toronto. He was on oxygen 24 hours a day with a limited life expectancy. He underwent right lung transplantation on November 7, 1983. He was discharged in 6 weeks and returned to work in 3 months. He died more than 7 years later of renal failure. The group at Freeman Hospital in

Newcastle-upon-Tyne, U.K. followed the path shown by the Toronto group and reported similar good outcome in patients with pulmonary fibrosis.

At the end of the 1990s lung transplants were infrequent and probably only considered when death was imminent. In this case watch this space in the next century.

Skin which I consider as grafts became very common and our local A & E had a doctor that not only recommended this for a major cut on my daughters hand but completed the process for me to get her home for Sunday lunch and for me to get to the afternoon bowls match. Everybody happy.

Intestine, heart valves, bone marrow and vascularized composite allografts were all significant at the end of the century with many success stories.

What magnificent progress in such a relevant short time and just how many patients profited from these developments. Wow!

Remedial Surgery/Medicine

First I will give you my bit of history by listing all the major advances that I have identified relating to the 1900s. This is really to give you an idea of the dramatic progress made in such a short time relative to everything that had gone on in the previous 1000 years. This will be followed by comments of interest and then I will divide into the separate areas of surgery and medicine

1900. About this time Harvey Cushing began pioneering brain surgery.

1901. German surgeon George Kelling performed the first Laparoscopic surgery on dogs. (Origins of keyhole surgery)

1901. Austrian physician Karl Landsteiner discovered the basic A-B-AB-O blood types.

1903. Dutch physician Willem Einthoven invented the Electrocardiograph.

1905. Novocaine was first used as a local anesthetic.

1907. Austrian surgeon Hermann Schloffer became the first to successfully remove a pituitary tumor.

1910. Swiss physician Hans Christian Jacobaeus performed the first Laparoscopic surgery on humans.

1914. Blood transfusion was pioneered.

1916. Austrian surgeon Hermann Schloffer performed the first splenectomy operation. (removal of the spleen)

1917. New Zealand surgeon Harold Gillies pioneered modern plastic surgery for wounded British World War I soldiers.

1925. The first open heart surgery by English surgeon Henry Souttar.

1929. Werner Forssmann performed the first cardiac catheterization, on himself.

1931. The first sex reassignment surgery.

1940. The first successful metallic hip replacement surgery

1948. The first successful open heart surgery operations since 1925.

1952. The first successful open heart surgery using hypothermia.

1953. The first carotid endarterectomy. (surgical removal of part of the inner lining of an artery)

1954. The first kidney transplant.

1955. The first artificial cardiac pacemaker.

1955. The first separation operation for conjoined twins.

1961. The cochlear implant was invented by William F. House.

1962. The first hip replacement surgery via Low Frictional Torque Arthroplasty.

1963. The first liver transplant was performed by Thomas Starzl et al.

1964. The laser scalpel was invented.

1967: The first successful heart transplant by Christiaan Barnard.

1967. The first successful coronary artery bypass surgery.

1972. The CT scan was perfected.

1982. The Jarvik-7 artificial heart was successfully installed.

1983. Robot-assisted surgery began in Vancouver.

1985. The first laparoscopic cholecystectomy by a German surgeon (keyhole surgery on a human)

1987. The first successful heart-lung transplant.

1998. The first Stem Cell Therapy.

In the 20th century, a number of these technologies have had a significant impact on surgical practice. Particularly Electrosurgery, practical Endoscopy beginning in the 1960s, and Laser surgery, Computer-assisted surgery and Robotic surgery, developed in the 1980s

The use of X-rays as an important medical diagnostic tool began with their discovery in 1895 by German physicist Wilhelm Röntgen. He noticed that these rays could penetrate the skin, allowing the skeletal structure to be captured on a specially treated photographic plate.

Advanced research centres opened in the early 20th century, often connected with major hospitals. The mid-20th century was characterized by new biological treatments, such as antibiotics. These advancements, along with developments in chemistry, genetics, and radiography led to modern medicine.
     The ABO blood group system was discovered in 1901, and the Rhesus blood group system in 1937, facilitating blood transfusion. During the 20th century Canadian physician Norman Bethune, M.D. developed a mobile blood-transfusion service for frontline operations in the Spanish Civil War (1936–1939), but ironically, he himself died of blood poisoning. Thousands of scarred troops provided the need for improved prosthetic limbs and expanded techniques in plastic surgery or reconstructive surgery. Those practices were combined to broaden cosmetic surgery and other forms of elective surgery.

During the second World War, Alexis Carrel and Henry Dakin developed the Carrel-Dakin method of treating wounds with an irrigation, Dakin's solution, a germicide which helped prevent gangrene.

The War spurred the usage of Roentgen's X-ray, and the electrocardiograph, for the monitoring of internal bodily functions. The advances in medicine made a dramatic difference for Allied troops, while the Germans and especially the Japanese and Chinese suffered from a severe lack of newer medicines, techniques and facilities. Surveys find that the chances of recovery for a badly wounded British infantryman were as much as 25 times better than in the First World War. The reason was that:

> "By 1944 most casualties were receiving treatment within hours of wounding, due to the increased mobility of field hospitals and the extensive use of aeroplanes as ambulances. The care of the sick and wounded had also been revolutionized by new medical technologies, such as active immunization against tetanus, sulphonamide drugs, and penicillin."

The World Health Organization was founded in 1948 as a United Nations agency to improve global health.

Starting in World War II, DDT was used as insecticide to combat insect vectors carrying malaria, which was endemic in most tropical regions of the world. The first goal was to protect soldiers, but it was widely adopted as a public health device. The World Health Organization (WHO) launched an antimalarial program in parts of Liberia as a pilot project to determine the feasibility of malaria eradication in tropical

Africa. However these projects encountered a spate of difficulties that foreshadowed the general retreat from malaria eradication efforts across tropical Africa by the mid-1960s.

A cochlear implant is a common kind of neural prosthesis.

Cancer treatment has been developed with radiotherapy, chemotherapy and surgical oncology.

Oral rehydration therapy has been extensively used since the 1970s to treat cholera and other diarrhea-inducing infections.

The sexual revolution included taboo-breaking research in human sexuality such as the 1948 and 1953 Kinsey reports, invention of hormonal contraception, and the normalization of abortion and homosexuality in many countries. Family planning has promoted a demographic transition in most of the world. With threatening sexually transmitted infections, not least HIV, use of barrier contraception has become imperative. The struggle against HIV has improved antiretroviral treatments.

X-ray imaging was the first kind of medical imaging, and later ultrasonic imaging, CT scanning, MR scanning and other imaging methods became available.

Evidence-based medicine is a modern concept, not introduced to literature until the 1990s.

In 1958, Arne Larsson in Sweden became the first patient to depend on an artificial cardiac pacemaker. He died in 2001 at age 86, having outlived its inventor, the surgeon, and 26 pacemakers. Lightweight materials as well as neural prosthetics emerged in the end of the 20th century.

Cardiac surgery was revolutionized in 1948 as open-heart surgery was introduced for the first time since 1925.

By the end of the 20th century, microtechnology had been used to create tiny robotic devices to assist microsurgery using micro-video and fiber-optic cameras to view internal tissues during surgery with minimally invasive practices.

Keyhole surgery was broadly introduced in the 1990s. Natural orifice surgery has followed. Remote surgery is another recent development.

Surgery.

 Coming back to what we all understand let us now consider the things we have seen happen around us in the 1900s. The advancement and success of the following processes really only came about as a result of the developments in medicine and photography (X-ray, CT scans etc.) described later but are mainly the result of anesthetics, steroids, cortisones and miniature cameras combined with computer technology.

Bones. Bones as well as being replaced have also been mended. The art of setting a shin bone for example was first to strap it and then later to splint it. I have always related this to getting sailors back to work on the old ships as there were no other facilities available, however, for everyone else plaster-of-Paris was apparently used as early as 1850. The real progress came when x-rays enabled doctors to assess the kind of break, particularly multiple breaks to joints, and to then make an appropriate casting.

Hernia. The most common hernia was to the groin and this was where, usually through excess strain, the stomach wall popped out through the protecting muscles. When this happened to me in the late fifties it was quite a serious operation and the surgeon made a large incision requiring 13 stitches/clips. He then had to pull the protrusion back from the muscles and snip them so that they were longer and would stop a reoccurrence. I was in hospital for two weeks. The doctor who signed me off for early retirement did not believe this version and told me I would need both hernias attended to within two years as they were 'loose'. At the end of the century nine years later I was still active and had not had need for an operation. My children have had different experiences as the modern method is to ease the hernia back and place a gauze in place to complete the process, this incurs a day's visit with no overnight stay. Unfortunately I hear of multiple returns to hospital for repeated surgery. Hiatus and other internal hernias still require a stay in hospital because they have to have intrusive surgery'

Ulcers have always been a serious problem because of the bleeding and poison in the stomach area but modern antibiotics particularly have made this problem usually manageable.

Gall Bladder and other stones in the intestines have always been extremely painful and were not always recommended for surgery but towards the end of the 1900s medicine and keyhole surgery made this a very much less onerous task.

Appendix (peritonitis) is actually only serious when infection bursts out. This was a case of call the ambulance and get the job done 'tout suite'. Again by the 90s there was a trend that said the operation could be avoided and only needed treating with the modern drugs. I think each case was then treated on its severity.

Verruca also wart is in the same class. This was quite common in the mid-century and often transferred, it is thought, in the swimming pool changing rooms. If treated early enough it could be handled with known medication but if this did not work it would become severe and need hospital treatment. This was done by applying liquid nitrogen to the affected spot in order to burn the wart out. With more chlorine being added to the water and better disinfection in the changing area this seems to be somewhat a thing of the past.

Obesity became recognized as a medical problem by the NHS and treatment became available, if you got the right recommendations, for free. The first operations, again based on family experience, was to stitch off half of the stomach and later do a further operation to remove excess fat. It was not long before this was taken off the free list and in our case the second operation did not get approval. Around the 90s the procedures were reintroduced as 'tummy tucks' as technology had improved. I have always felt that this was in truth a short term success story as given time and lack of dedication the stomach grew back to its original capacity. Result! The person becomes obese.

Laser Eye. In the 1930s, long before the advent of laser eye surgery, Dr Sato in Japan was the first to introduce vision correction surgery. He used a scalpel to make incisions on the inside surface of the cornea that would radiate out, rather like slicing a pizza. His technique appeared successful at first, but ultimately failed, and all his patients had to have corneal grafts.

Vision correction development pre laser eye surgery came along in the 1970s. In Moscow, Dr Fyoderov used a similar technique, although this time on the front surface of the cornea. The technique, which he called 'radial keratotomy', allowed the steep myopic cornea to flatten and re-shape in the centre.

The laser eye surgery story actually began with microchips. In 1980, an IBM scientist was busy operating an excimer laser while producing circuits in microchips for information equipment when it occurred to him that the laser could also cut organic tissue without creating damage to the surrounding tissue.

During the 1980s, experiments into how to best utilise technology to perform laser eye surgery continued around the world at a hot pace. A book could be written on what was being discovered during this time, although some of the most notable events included:

1983 – New York ophthalmologist, Dr Steven Trokel, discovered the ability to re-shape the cornea with an excimer laser

1984 – Laser experiments on animals indicate that corneal tissue could be removed without leaving a scar

1985 – London ophthalmologist, John Marshall, recognised that the tissue needed to be removed from the cornea in the shape of a disc, rather than the radiating lines the others were working on and PRK was born.

1985 – Dr Theo Seiler performs the first excimer laser procedure (PRK) on a human patient in Dresden

1988 – Dr Marguerite McDonald performed the first PRK laser eye surgery procedure on a healthy eye in New Orleans, Louisiana

1989 – Greek ophthalmologist, Ionnis Pallikaris, conceived the technique now known as LASIK, where a flap is raised in the cornea prior to laser eye surgery.

Here is just another example of my having personal experience. In this case one of our bridesmaids was born with a known eye impairment. She attended Moorfields Hospital in London, which was one of, if not, the leading eye specialist's in the world. In the late 1980s her surgeon told her that it had got to a stage where surgery was the only option left that might help her retain some sight. She was living in Wales at the time so on the appointed date she stayed overnight with us and I took her to the hospital early next morning. We had all worked up to handling the occasion but when she met her surgeon he said that he felt the odds of success were so bad that she should savor what she had for another year. Whether he knew more than he was saying I will never know. The truth is that a year later we went through the whole rigmarole all over again (me getting her drunk on Irish coffee) and taking her to Moorfields. This time though she rang us in the early afternoon and said she had just spoken to her brother and that she was going over to see him that evening. She really did mean see him as she had had this new-fangled surgery and it was in her words successful.

In practice it actually restored only a percentage of her sight but it was more than enough for her to see the full features of her last born which had not previously been possible.

Medicines.

This section will be considered in three categories; curative, containing and preventative, that is, they are regarded as **Curative**, if they actually ease pain assist or actually repair an ill, as **Containing** if they assist the body to improve or replicate a failed function, or as **Preventative** if they are statistically or otherwise considered to reduce the risk of recurrent or related illness.

Curative

Antibiotics. Imagine a world without antibiotics. A cut to your finger could leave you fighting for your life.

Before antibiotics, medics used various measures to protect against disease-causing bacteria. Strict hygiene was universally important and individual treatments were used for specific illnesses. For example, tuberculosis, a bacterial infection of the lungs, could only be treated with fresh air and rest.

As bacteria gain the ability to resist the effects of our antibiotic drugs and no new drugs are developed, our past could become our future. Without antibiotics many medical procedures would not be possible, including clean surgery and organ transplantation, chemotherapy for cancer patients and care for premature babies.

Penicillin was not the first antibiotic. Before the work of Howard Florey and his team, other drugs had already revolutionised the treatment of infections. <u>Salvarsan</u> was produced in Germany by the medical scientist Paul Ehrlich to treat syphilis. In 1909 Ehrlich used the phrase 'magic bullet' to describe this new wonder drug. It became one of the most prescribed drugs in the world, though the bacteria that caused syphilis quickly started to develop resistance to the treatment.

During the 1930s, chemists in Germany, France, and Britain discovered a whole range of new and effective chemical antibiotics. These drugs were called sulphonamides; they revolutionised the treatment of previously deadly bacterial infections.

The sulphonamide M&B 693 was developed in Britain and first prescribed in 1938 to treat pneumonia. The most famous patient saved by the drug was British Prime Minister Winston Churchill, who contracted pneumonia at the height of the Second World War. The drug most likely saved his life and the success of the treatment was widely reported in the press.

This original laboratory sample of M&B 693 was produced by May and Baker of Dagenham.

By the end of the 1900s antibiotics were widely used not only by doctors but dentists also regularly prescribed them to clear up infections prior to removing a tooth. (I still do not understand why if they have cured an infection there is still a need to remove the tooth. My guess is that it is fear of a recurrence).

Another one of my asides is that in about 1943 my brother was particularly ill and the doctor prescribed M & B tablets which none of us had ever heard of.

Later in June 1947 I was rushed to the ENT hospital in Holborn, London for an operation on my very painful ear. We arrived at not long before midnight and a surgeon was waiting for us. He prepared for the procedure but just after he had administered the gas to put me out, all of the lights fused. He proceeded to mend the fuse, scrub up and then with me barely asleep performed the op. I was awake immediately after he had finished when he offered to carry me to the nearest men's ward. Next day when I told my story to the nurse she was absolutely aghast. This did not stop them keeping me there for the next two weeks and every four hours, on the dot, administer a vicious jab of penicillin. Yes you did not get a simple pill but what felt like a very large needle for the whole fourteen days.

Steroids (short for corticosteroids) and, here I include Cortisone, are synthetic drugs that closely resemble cortisol, a hormone that your body produces naturally. Steroids work by decreasing inflammation and reducing the activity of the immune system. They are used to treat a variety of inflammatory diseases and conditions

The first clinical evidence that an extract of animal adrenocortical tissue could counteract human adrenal failure was demonstrated in 1930. As chemical analyses of cortical extracts proceeded, it became evident that there is not one cortical hormone, but that all are steroids. By 1940 it was understood that there are two categories: those that cause sodium and fluid retention and those that counteract shock and inflammation. Structurally the presence or lack of oxygenation on the steroid skeleton was critical. In 1948 the first patient with rheumatoid arthritis was treated with cortisone and soon thereafter other rheumatologic patients received cortisone. Oral and intra-articular administration of cortisone and hydrocortisone began in 1950-51. Several lines of research to produce cortisone semi-synthetically showed some success by 1952. Between 1954 and 1958 six synthetic steroids were introduced for systemic anti-inflammatory therapy. By 1960 all of the toxic effects of chronic corticosteroid administration had been described, identifying dangers of large or long term use. To enable use of lower corticosteroid dosages, companion use of non-steroidal anti-inflammatory drugs began in the late 1950s, with phenylbutazone the first. In the 1970s the introduction of methotrexate and other anti-metabolites further circumscribed the dosages and indications for corticosteroids in the rheumatic diseases.

Common known steroids are:

Prednisolone is always prescribed for severe attacks of various asthma (bronchial etc.) and rheumatic (e.g. polymyalgia) problems

Testosterone was first synthesized in Germany in 1935 and was used medically to treat depression. Professional athletes began misusing anabolic steroids during the 1954 Olympics, when Russian weightlifters were given testosterone.

Cortisone as a general drug is commonly given for things like tennis elbow and other dubiously identified pains. I have always felt that it was used to cover up pain rather than cure a specific problem and was admonished by a rheumatoid surgeon.

Other Painkillers. These do not necessarily cure but often provide the body with the chance to self-cure by relieving pain and relaxing the muscles.

Aspirin. The aspirin we know came into being in the late 1890s in the form of acetylsalicylic acid when chemist Felix Hoffmann at Bayer in Germany used it to alleviate his father's rheumatism, a timeline from Bayer says. Beginning in 1899, Bayer distributed a powder with this ingredient to physicians to give to patients. The drug became a hit and, in 1915, it was sold as over-the-counter tablets.
One patient who should not have been taking aspirin was young, and had haemophilia, Aspirin would make the bleeding in this disorder worse, which is why it was later decided to limit the dosage in some cases and introduce a complimentary drug to the medication.
A half aspirin a day for life was prescribed for life after heart surgery.

Paracetamol. This mild pain reliever has a history that dates back to 1893. This was the first time it got clinical use. It wasn't available for commercial use in the United States until 1950. Australia started using it commercially in 1956. Originally sold under the name Triagesic, this drug was a combination of paracetamol, caffeine, and aspirin.

After the initial introduction in 1950, the manufacturers removed it from commercial use until 1953. The Sterling-Winthrop Company began marketing it under the name Panadol. You could only get Paracetamol by prescription until 1959. It then switched to an over-the-counter medication. From the 1960s to the 1980s, the drug's popularity increased rapidly. It is now considered to be a household drug. Any patents have expired and there are dozens of generic versions of Paracetamol available today.

Opiates, originally derived from the opium poppy, have been used for thousands of years for both recreational and medicinal purposes. The most active substance in opium is morphine—named after Morpheus, the Greek god of dreams.

Morphine is a very powerful painkiller, but it is also very addictive.

In the sixteenth century, laudanum, opium prepared in an alcoholic solution, was used as a painkiller.

Morphine was first extracted from opium in a pure form in the early nineteenth century. It was used widely as a painkiller during the American Civil War, and many soldiers became addicted.

Throughout the early nineteenth century, the recreational use of opium grew and by 1830, the British dependence on the drug reached an all-time high. The British sent warships to the coast of China in 1839 in response to China's attempt to suppress the opium traffic, beginning the "First Opium War."

In 1874, chemists trying to find a less addictive form of morphine made heroin. But **heroin** had twice the potency of morphine, and heroin addiction soon became a serious problem.

The US Congress banned opium in 1905 and the next year passed the Pure Food and Drug Act requiring contents labelling on all medicines.

Methadone was first synthesized in 1937 by German scientists Max Bockmühl and Gustav Ehrhart. They were searching for a painkiller that would be easier to use during surgery, with less addiction potential than morphine or heroin.

Methadone is, however, believed by many to be even more addictive than heroin.

Meanwhile, the illegal opium trade boomed. By 1995, Southeast Asia was producing 2,500 tons annually.

New painkillers came on the market with approval from the Food and Drug Administration: **Vicodin** in 1984, **OxyContin** in 1995 and **Percocet** in 1999.

These are all synthetic (man-made) opiates which mimic (imitate) the body's own painkillers

Codeine is a less powerful drug that is found in opium but can be synthesized (man-made), was first isolated in 1830 in France by Jean-Pierre Robiquet, to replace raw opium for medical purposes.

All opiates temporarily relieve pain but are highly addictive.

Anti-inflammatories. These often work in conjunction with the painkillers which might inflame the stomach but are also used for addressing specific problems.

Containing

As implied previously are life-saving or at least life-extending and none of these existed at the start of the 1900s.

Insulin is now commonly understood to be the only and successful treatment for Type 1 diabetes. True, or just an old wives tale, around the 1920s spinach was reputed to be the only diet that managed diabetes and it had to make up most of the food intake.

Before 1921, it was exceptional for people with Type 1 diabetes to live more than a year or two. One of the twentieth century's greatest medical discoveries, it remains the only effective treatment for people with Type 1 diabetes today

Insulin was discovered by Sir Frederick G Banting, Charles H Best and JJR Macleod at the University of Toronto in 1921 and it was subsequently purified by James B Collip.

In January 1922, Leonard Thompson, a 14-year-old boy dying from diabetes in a Toronto hospital, became the first person to receive an injection of insulin. About this time I understand that it was not unknown for wards of up to 50 children being kept together just waiting to die (most in a coma). One of the early pioneers arranged to go through one of these wards and inject each child in turn with insulin. By the time he got to the last child the first injected were already coming out of their comas to the delight of the grieving parents.

The first genetically engineered, synthetic "human" insulin was produced in 1978 using E. coli bacteria to produce the insulin.

Thyroid The goal of treating hypothyroidism is to replace the deficient thyroid hormone. This is done with oral medication, using the synthetic thyroid hormone thyroxine (T4) or levothyroxine. This treatment is proven to be safe and effective with more consistent results.

Levothyroxine was first made in 1927. It is on the World Health Organization's List of Essential Medicines, the safest and most effective medicines needed in a health system. Levothyroxine is available as a generic medication.

Water Pills. In the mid-1950s the first modern diuretic, acetazolamide, a powerful carbonic anhydrase inhibitor, was developed (first generation). In the late 1950s and in the

1960s, a significant break- through was achieved with the discovery of chlorothiazide, furosemide and ethacrynic acid (second generation). Many patients are often surprised to find out they can actually drink too much water as they have been instructed that drinking lots of water is the key to staying healthy. Many patients take diuretics to help reduce fluid retention but it is still important to follow the fluid restriction recommended by the physician

Pacemaker This is included here although it is strictly not a medicine. I mentioned it in the heart surgery discussions but this is somewhat unique and deserves special attention. Wilson Greatbatch, an American electrical engineer, invented the first implantable cardiac pacemaker, in 1958.

The advantages of pacing the heart electrically were well known as far back as the early 1900s. Early pacemakers were large, bulky external devices that used vacuum tubes, relied on external ac power, and were frequently too traumatic for young patients. It wasn't until shortly after Medtronic was founded that significant progress began.

Earl Bakken and his brother-in-law Palmer Hermundslie formed Medtronic in April 1949 as a medical equipment service company. Both men conceived the idea of the cardiac pacemaker while Bakken was working part time at Northwestern Hospital in Minneapolis, Minn.

It wasn't until late 1959, when Dr William Chardack and Dr Andrew, working with electrical engineer William Greatbatch, came up with a viable implantable pacemaker using primary cells (Greatbatch also inventing the necessary tiny lithium-iodine battery) as a power source. It was known as the

Chardack-Greatbatch implantable pacemaker and through his company Greatbatch Enterprises, licensed his patent to Medtronic in 1961.

Pacemakers were made non-invasively programmable in the mid-1970s. Using a radio-frequency telemetry link, most pacing parameters could be adjusted to follow the changing clinical needs of the patient. By the end of the 70's dual-chamber pacemakers were developed to pace and sense in both atria and ventricles. Synchronised timing made it possible to preserve the atrial contribution to ventricular filling as well as to track the intrinsic atrial rate.

In the mid-1980s rate-responsive pacemakers were designed. A tiny sensor within the pacemaker box detected body movement and used this as a surrogate measure of activity. Signals from the sensor were filtered and applied to an algorithm to alter the pacing rate up or down. Thus, pacing rate would change according to the patient's activity level.

By the mid-80's fitting cardiac pacemakers had become a routine procedure which saved thousands of lives

In the1990s Microprocessor-driven pacemakers appeared. These became very complex devices capable of detecting and storing events utilising several algorithms. They delivered therapy and modified their internal pacing parameters according to the changing needs of the patient in an automatic manner. The rate-response pattern also adjusted itself automatically to the patient's activity level.

I find this one of the amazing stories of the century and felt I must share it here to impress on you how people and development has so outrun all natural expectation.

Preventative

Medicine is not, as you will have realised, high on my list of 'goodies', as I have referred previously to not making them free on the NHS and to not personally be keen on using them. These are justified on the basis that they, by possible prevention, extend life or at the other end of the spectrum, prevent birth. This is too general and to bigoted to be fair so I will just list and qualify the main known mendicants.

Statins. (Cholesterol lowering drugs). Lovastatin, a compound isolated from Aspergillus terreus, was the first statin to be marketed. Statins, also known as HMG-CoA reductase inhibitors, are a class of lipid-lowering medications that reduce the chance of illness and mortality in those who are at high risk of cardiovascular disease.

In the 1950s and 1960s, it became obvious that elevated concentrations of plasma cholesterol represent a major risk factor for the development of heart disease, which led to the quest for drugs that could reduce it.

While working at the Sankyo Company in 1976, the Japanese biochemist Akira Endo isolated a factor from the fungus Penicillium citrinum which he identified as a competitive inhibitor. This substance, which he named compactin or mevastatin, was the first statin to be administered to humans.

Clinical studies of compactin in Japan ensued soon after that, as well as experimental studies around the world. In 1978, Alfred Alberts with his colleagues at Merck Research Laboratories discovered a potent inhibitor of HMG-CoA reductase in a fermentation broth of Aspergillus terreus, which was named lovastatin, mevinolin or monacolin K.

Since lovastatin has been commercialized, six statins – including two semi-synthetic statins (known as simvastatin and pravastatin) and three synthetic statins (fluvastatin, rosuvastatin and pitavastatin) – have been introduced to the market.

So should you take statins? The short answer is, don't start, if you haven't had a heart attack that is. Here are five quick reasons why not

1) The statistics. If statins were in a horse race you wouldn't even consider betting on them. The simple fact is that the odds you are going to benefit are lousy. As in other gambling situations even the experts don't agree on the exact odds, but the Lancet paper – and it says this is a good bet – puts your chances of avoiding a "serious vascular event" such as a heart attack or a heart operation, at 167 to 1 – if you are healthy with a low risk that is. And you have to keep taking them for five years. Other studies have come up with figures that are even worse. Another found that if 10,000 people, who were healthy but at high risk, took statins for four years there was no evidence they would live any longer. The study did find 7 fewer deaths in the statin group but said that the number was so small it wasn't statistically significant.

2 The side-effects. Because the chances of benefitting personally are so small, it becomes very important to know your chance of suffering side effects. Here there is even less agreement among the experts. Muscle damage has always been a concern but while the evidence from trials puts it at about 1% others, especially, clinicians who see patients on a daily basis put it far higher maybe up to 20%. And this isn't just unpleasant, it can seriously interfere with your ability to exercise, one of the best ways of avoiding heart disease. There is also a big debate going on about statins raising the risk of diabetes. They might give you a 200 to one risk of developing it – pretty close to the benefits.

3 The missing enzyme. The big statin trials never mention that statins as well as cutting cholesterol also block production of this substance that is vital for the effective working of muscles – the heart is a muscle, and for producing energy . In Canada statin packets come with a warning about this and advice to supplement.

4 Learn to love your cholesterol. Cholesterol has a number of important functions in your body, so it seems wise not to lower it without good reason and a 1 in 167 possibility of benefit doesn't seem that good. It is part of the membrane surrounding each brain cell, 20% of our total cholesterol is found in the brain, where it controls, among other things, the transmission of message through the nerve cells. One of the commonly reported statin side effects is memory loss and brain fog. Cholesterol is also the feedstock that the body uses to make all our sex hormones

5 It's the lifestyle stupid. Even the most ardent statin supporters pay lip service to the benefits of changing your lifestyle, eating well, exercising and so on. But doctors are not particularly good at helping you to do that – making those sorts of changes is hard and you need support – so drugs are the easy option. But a trial involving 20,000 people found making just four of the most basic lifestyle changes – stopping smoking, drinking moderately, exercising and eating five-a-day fruit and vegetables – put an astonishing 14 years onto their life span. Compared that with going for a 167 to one chance of avoiding a heart attack and the choice really is a no brainer.

I do not know which newspaper or magazine that I read this in but one of the doctors that write in my daily newspaper would wholeheartedly agree and probably find more reasons to add to the list, e.g. Statins can cause gas, diarrhoea, nausea, and other digestive track troubles.

Beta-blockers are drugs that block the effects of adrenaline, the hormone that triggers your body's fight-or-flight response when you're stressed. This slows your heart rate and eases up on the force your heart squeezes. Your blood pressure goes down because your heart isn't working so hard. These medicines can also relax blood vessels so the blood flows better hopefully extending life expectancy.

Blood Thinners. Up to the end of the 20th century there was really only one prescribed blood thinner (Warfarin). If you have ever doubted that pharmacologically potent compounds can be derived from plants, consider the history of warfarin. In the 1920s cattle in the Northern USA and Canada were afflicted by an outbreak of an unusual disease, characterised by fatal bleeding, either spontaneously or from minor injuries. Mouldy silage made from sweet clover was implicated, however, it was not until 1940 that Karl Link and his student Harold Campbell in Wisconsin discovered the anticoagulant properties in sweet clover. Further work in 1948 resulted in warfarin being approved as a rodenticide in the USA in 1952, and then for human use in 1954.

Warfarin is now the most widely used anticoagulant in the world. Given the demise of ximelagatran, the first oral thrombin inhibitor, it is likely to maintain its place for many years to come. In the UK it has been estimated that at least 1% of the whole population and 8% of those aged over 80 years are taking warfarin. The increase in its use can undoubtedly be traced to overwhelming evidence of its effectiveness in preventing embolic strokes in patients with atrial fibrillation. I question whether this is statistics or real science.

The main adverse effect associated with warfarin is bleeding. Major and fatal bleeding events occur respectively at rates of 7.2 and 1.3 per 100 patient-years, according to a meta-analysis of 33 studies. Warfarin is also number three on the list of drugs implicated in causing hospital admission through adverse effects. Warfarin's narrow therapeutic index makes it difficult to maintain patients within a defined anticoagulation range. The problem is further compounded by the fact that individual dosage requirements vary widely between and within individuals.

The usual model of care of patients taking anticoagulants involves attendance at a physician-run hospital-based clinic.

Warfarin is associated with other adverse effects, including skin necrosis and hair loss.

So where are we heading with warfarin prescribing? Warfarin will continue to be the oral anticoagulant of choice this century, while we await an oral thrombin inhibitor that is both effective and safe. One of the mainstays of current treatment, enoxaparin, first emerged in 1987. LMWHs do not require monitoring and have lower risk, but they must be administered by injection, and can accumulate in patients with kidney impairment.

Not a glowing recommendation for a preventative only drug but as at the end of the 1900s the choice is follow your doctor advice or gamble.

Blood Pressure. It is surprising that only about the 1950s that hypertension was still considered an essential malady and not a treatable condition. Introduction of thiazide diuretics in late 50s made some headway in successful treatment of hypertension. Hypertension, however, was not always considered a disease as we know it now. President Franklin D. Roosevelt was given a clean bill of health by his physician even when his BP was recorded as ~220/120. A few years later while at Yalta, Winston Churchill's personal physician noted in his diary that President Roosevelt "appeared to be have had signs of 'hardening of the arteries disease' and had a few months to live." Subsequent events demonstrated the truth of his diagnosis. President Roosevelt ultimately had a fatal haemorrhagic stroke 2 months later, and his death brought hypertension's potential as a deadly malady to the limelight. His treatment had consisted of phenobarbital, a low-fat, low-sodium diet, and rest, there was little else that was available as effective treatment at that time.

List of Available Antihypertensive Drugs. From the 1930s to the end of the century.

1930s   Veratrum alkaloids

1940s   Thiocyanates

        Ganglion blocking agents

        Catecholamine depletors (Rauwolfia derivatives)

1950s   Vasodilators (Hydralazine)

        Peripheral sympathetic inhibitors (guanethidine)

        Monoamine oxidase inhibitors

        Diuretics

1960s   Central $\alpha2$-agonists (sympathetic nervous system inhibitors)

        β-Adrenergic inhibitors

1970 α-Adrenergic inhibitors

        α-β-Blockers

        Converting enzyme inhibitors

1980s   Calcium channel blockers

1990s   Angiotensin II (AT1) receptor antagonists

In the 1960s we were still using medications that caused numerous side effects

Large clinical trials were mounted in the 1960s to 1980s to demonstrate, if possible, the benefits of therapy in less severe degrees of hypertension.

Using combinations of small doses of different classes of drugs increased response rates and reduced side effects.

British literature in the mid-late 1970s was advising physicians that Antihypertensive agents produce no obvious benefit in patients just over 65.

Hypotensive drugs should probably not be given (in the elderly) unless the blood pressure is more than 200/110 mm Hg.24.

Over the years, as more information became available, more vigorous therapy was recommended at lower levels of pressure. The JNC V, published in 1993, changed definitions of hypertension to highlight the importance of systolic blood pressure as a major risk factor for heart disease. Persistent blood pressures > 140/90 mm Hg in the young or the elderly adult were now considered indications for treatment. The lowering of blood pressure with antihypertensive agents had been shown to reduce morbidity and mortality in middle-aged and older individuals and the benefits of treatment clearly outweighed the risks even in less severe cases.

Combination therapy with small doses of two different drugs is now accepted as a reasonable treatment approach to achieve blood pressure lowering with fewer side effects.

Rather than medication to control the blood pressure there are some simple recommendations:

Exercise most days of the week. Exercise is the most effective way to lower your blood pressure.

Consume a low-sodium diet. Too much sodium (or salt) causes blood pressure to rise.

Limit alcohol intake to no more than 1 to 2 drinks per day.

Make stress reduction a priority.

This diatribe emphasises how difficult it is to identify and then resolve a perceived medical condition. Through the back end of the century there was a lot of hard work and relatively slow progress. In truth the progress was excellent when compared to previous centuries but appeared to pale when compared to the dramatic advances in many other areas of medical research. But this still begs the question is the search for preventative medicine really progress. I think in this case the answer will come early in the 21st century.

Anti-depressants. Antidepressant drugs are as controversial as they are popular. And, my, are they popular.

Researchers discovered the first antidepressants purely by chance in the 1950s. Seeking a treatment for schizophrenia, scientists at the Munsterlingen asylum in Switzerland found that a drug that tweaked the balance of the brain's neurotransmitters — the chemicals that control mood, pain and other sensations — sent patients into bouts of euphoria. For schizophrenics, of course, that only made their condition worse. But researchers soon realized it made their pill perfect for patients with depression. On first trying it in 1955, some patients found themselves newly sociable and energetic and called the drug a "miracle cure." The drug, called imipramine and marketed as Tofranil in 1958, was quickly followed by dozens of rivals — known as tricyclics for their three-ring chemical structure.

The drugs provided relief to 60% to 80% of patients, but they also caused serious side effects, including sluggishness, weight gain and occasionally death from overdose. The ground was ripe for a better pill, and it wasn't long before scientists produced a new, highly targeted class of antidepressants, led by Prozac in 1987, followed by Zoloft in 1991 and Paxil in 1992.

By 1993, Prozac had been taken by some 10 million people around the globe. In contrast to the obscure antidepressants of generations past, Newsweek noted in 1994, "Prozac has attained the familiarity of Kleenex and the social status of spring water." Depression had begun to shake its stigma.

These drugs have taken flight and soared far beyond the depressed patients for whom they were initially approved. Doctors have prescribed them to everyone from pensioners to preteens for everything from PMS to fear of public speaking. Prozac is used even in veterinary medicine, for dogs that seem down in the dumps.

They can also be used to treat a number of other conditions, including:

Obsessive compulsive disorder (OCD)

Generalised anxiety disorder

Post-traumatic stress disorder (PTSD)

Antidepressants are also sometimes used to treat people with long-term (chronic) pain.

The side effects of antidepressants can cause problems at first, but then generally improve with time.

It's important to continue treatment, even if you're affected by side effects, as it will take several weeks before you begin to benefit from treatment. With time, you should find that the benefits of treatment outweigh any problems from side effects.

During the first few months of treatment, you'll usually see your doctor or a specialist nurse at least once every 2 to 4 weeks to see how well the medicine is working

Children and young people with moderate to severe depression should first be offered a course of psychotherapy that lasts for at least 3 months. In some cases, an SSRI called fluoxetine may be offered in combination with psychotherapy to treat moderate to severe depression in young people aged 12 to 18.

I believe the foregoing has come from reputable sources and that in the U K a significant number of school children are regularly being prescribe Prozac for OCD. The combination of drugs and psychotherapy, particularly in young people always strikes me as a 'cop out' and that the parents and doctors are giving in too frequently to tantrums which are now considered an illness. Along the way I have heard parents say that the problem comes from a fizzy diet or wrong sleep patterns etc. but I think parents and schools should work harder and not turn to the over worked G P. I guess that here again I am not overly enamoured with preventative rather than pro-active treatments.

Antihistamine. In some humans, the immune system perceives irritants such as pollen or animal dander to be foreign substances dangerous to the body. When these are inhaled into the body, antibodies seek out the irritant and combine with it. A large blood cell known as a basophil, or mast cell, then releases the compound histamine, which attaches itself to receptor cells in mucous membranes. Histamine then causes the local blood vessels to dilate. A drop in blood pressure and increased permeability of the vessel walls also occurs, allowing fluids from the blood to escape into surrounding tissues. These reactions are responsible for the itching, "runny nose," and "watery eyes" of a cold or hay fever, as histamines attempt to rid the body of the irritant.

By 1942 the first antihistamine successfully used to treat humans, Antergan, was developed in France. Antergan was revised to Neo-Antergan in 1944. Scientists in the United States introduced diphenhydramine and tripellinamine in 1946, both of which remained in use through the end of the century.

By 1950 antihistamines were mass-produced and prescribed extensively as the drug of choice for those suffering from allergies (particularly hay-fever but also, skin, food, pet, and dust allergies, and insect bites and itchy skin). Hailed as "wonder drugs," antihistamines were often mistakenly perceived by the public as a cure for the common cold. Although not a cure, antihistamines provided the first dependable relief for some of the cold's symptoms.

Patients taking antihistamines experienced side effects that affected their daily activities of life. Studies indicated that one third of patients receiving antihistamines experienced drowsiness substantial enough to impair their concentration.

Patients were encouraged to time doses according to their own schedules and body rhythms to minimize side effects, rather than adhering to a rigid schedule.

Despite the side effects, antihistamines have become widely used in medicine at the turn of the twenty-first century which is a testament to the importance of Daniel Bovet's discovery.

This is one of the preventative drugs that has proved particularly successful but in this case it is not trying to stop a life threatening decease but to control and allergy. Anyway a good thing.

Type 2 Diabetes. There are two main types of diabetes: type 1 and type 2. People with type 1 diabetes don't produce insulin. Injecting insulin is the only known and proven treatment. People with type 2 diabetes don't respond to insulin as well as they should and later in the disease often don't make enough insulin.

Although there's no cure for type 2 diabetes, studies show it's possible for some people to reverse it.

So how can you reverse diabetes? The key seems to be weight loss. Not only can shedding pounds help you manage your diabetes, sometimes losing enough weight could help you live diabetes-free, especially if you've only had the disease for a short time and haven't needed insulin.

This doesn't mean you're completely cured. Type 2 diabetes is an ongoing disease. Even if you're in remission, which means you aren't taking medication and your blood sugar levels stay in a healthy range, there's always a chance that symptoms will return. But it's possible for some people to go years without trouble controlling their glucose and the health concerns that come with diabetes.

Diabetic parameters for diagnosis (and here I do break my rules and quote figures well into the early 2000s) are:

HbA1c	mmol/mol	%
Normal	below 42 mmol/mol	below 6.0%
Prediabetes	42 to 47 mmol/mol	6.0% to 6.4%
Diabetes	48 mmol/mol or over	6.5% or over

Medication for type 2 is normally one or more Metformin (Glucophage, Glumetza, others) pills.

Asthma. Salbutamol, also known as albuterol and marketed as Ventolin among other brand names, is a medication that opens up the medium and large airways in the lungs. It is used to treat asthma, including asthma attacks, exercise-induced bronchoconstriction, and chronic obstructive pulmonary disease. Most people recognise the Ventolin 'blue inhaler'.

The last two headings are actually referenced by the decease and not the preventative medicine because both of these are treated in similar styles by the medical profession in that the diagnosis is based on very little time and essence and, medication is given without significant follow-up procedures. I base this broad brush comment on my experiences. With the schoolchild asthma the press and unions appeared to want to get on to a bandwagon. The result was that we were later advised that asthma was over diagnosed and that many of the children had temporary respiratory problems. With type 2 diabetes I must do a little personal history. In 1989 while in a diabetic clinic I was told that one had diabetes if the HbA1c was less than 4 or greater than 9. This was, at that time, tested over several consultations and a number of tests. I understand that the less than 4 is still considered relevant but that the top figure in some clinics is regarded as no more than 6. I have witnessed blood sugars change dramatically in minutes as a result of changing circumstances and on a regular basis for a type 1 diabetic it can move as many as 8 points within half an hour. The figure before a meal is expected to be as much as 2 points lower than after.

Current perceived wisdom is that there are no known cures for these and I feel that instead of giving what appear to be cures which are actually medication for life, they should spend more time on education and fuller identification. Particularly with millions of diagnoses for pre and type 2 diabetes the significance of the type 1 strain is not always apparent to the general public and as a result they are careless about the need for good controls and proceed up the scale of illness. We hear of many people who are reported to have died from diabetes but the truth is it is not really the diabetes but a side effect that they have died from. This is usually the result of poor control which comes from the lack of respect for the seriousness of the decease. Could this be because we have so many diagnosed diabetics that they ignore the facts and think if all those millions can cope and cheat on their medication then I must be able to get away with it. I know I mentioned this in the politics but I must say that this time and money spent on Ventolin, metformin and follow-up clinics could be redirected to better purposes like medical science.

That officially concludes my history of medical progress during the 1900s but at this point I feel it is appropriate to say that what I have learnt in writing this is the astounding progress that has taken place. To illustrate this I will quote a few of the things that were accepted in the general way of life in 1900 that would now be treated almost as myth by the kids born in the 1990s.

Stillbirth and Infant death. It was common place for mothers to bear as many as 13 children but to then have a family of no more than 7.

Mobility. People limping and using walking sticks was commonplace. Broken bones were badly set and hip operations were pie in the sky.

Longevity. Life expectancy was no more than 60 years in the healthy areas and much less, say 40 plus in Glasgow.

Small Pox and Scarlet were killer deceases.

No Insulin. Diabetes was untreatable.

Gangrene could kill within minutes or at most hours and was rarely treatable.

Whatever! I still think that happiness is the best medicine

CHAPTER 4

TRANSPORT

I will deal this on two levels, when applicable, first the evolutional progress from the vehicular (Trains, Cars, Bikes etc.) available in 1900 to the space age later in the century. Secondly the social impact upon people's way of life; from local family changes and commercial benefits to seaside holidays to global travel.

Bikes - Evolution. These were at first essentially just two wheels and a fixed cog mostly attached via a chain to pedals. A prime example of this was the penny-farthing which did not have a chain but the pedals were attached directly to the very large front wheel. These were used to move around quicker to and from shops or occupation and for leisure or exercise. With the invention of the ball bearing it was not long before gearing was developed which made the comfort of cycling considerably better. Going uphill was more manageable and it was no longer necessary to push the bike on steep inclines. Also by using the gears wisely you could gain a considerably higher speed. From the original five or six miles an hour it became possible to travel at up to 29 mph. At that time the bikes were made of tubular steel. As lighter metals became available and cycle racing became popular the top speeds increased and by the 1950s the aim was to complete a twenty five mile race in under an hour. By the end of the century I think the first fifty mile race was completed in under two hours. In the early sixties my cousin and his wife were stopped by the police for breaking the speed limit in a built-up area.

They were actually too embarrassed to take them to the nick and charge them so just let them off with a warning. Cycling at purpose built tracks became popular and cycling was included as an Olympic sport.

The bike itself was pedal powered but it was not long before a small version of the motor car engine was developed and geared to power two wheels and this was the birth of the modern motor cycle.

Bikes – Social Impact. Starting late in the 1800 the bike was to have a big social impact and the following is an attempt to put the century into some perspective.

The bicycle craze boosted the "rational clothing" movement, which encouraged women to do away with long, cumbersome skirts and bulky undergarments. Safety bicycle frames accommodated skirts, which got shorter, and the most daring women chose bloomers that resembled men's pants.

For decades the bicycle was an important means of transport, though this changed with the economic boom of the 1950s. Motorbikes and cars quickly took hold and the only people who rode bikes were those who couldn't afford a motor vehicle or those who didn't have a driving licence or found it more convenient, when commuting, than other public transport.

Bicycle riding came to embody the individuality women were working toward with the suffrage movement. It also gave women a mode of transportation and clothing that allowed for freedom of movement and of travel.

It was easy to find cycling fascinating and photographs in the early 1900s showed stern men possessing suitably stiff upper lips, using their machines to journey off in the countryside, appreciate nature, visit cider farms and engage in dalliances with landladies' daughters.

One quote I found noted 'We have had many pleasures in the way of travelling, but we have never yet experienced such exhilarating enthusiasm or such complete recreation. What once was impossible has become possible, and distance is no longer the barrier to the refreshment of country life or contact with kindred spirits'.

One unexpected change to life was in the field of genetics. For the majority of those living in rural areas, owning a bicycle dramatically increased the number of potential marriage partners, as for the first time they possessed their own means of travelling beyond their local communities. The widening of gene pools which resulted from this process means that the biologist Steve Jones ranks the invention of the bicycle as the most important event in recent human evolution.

However, the most noticeable social change brought about by the bicycle was in the lives of women. At first, most female cyclists were from middle-class backgrounds, but as the price of bicycles decreased as the 1900s progressed, it became increasingly possible for working-class women to purchase machines.

Apart from the social side of cycling it also became a sport. Track cycling is particularly popular in Europe, notably Belgium, France, Germany and the United Kingdom where it is often used as off-season training by road racers who can frequently be seen at professional six-day events (races entered by two-rider teams).

Changes to bikes and how they impacted lives through the century include:

1903 Bikes became geared and chained and women could wear long skirts.

Throughout the century cycle velodromes were designed over various lengths and with variable banking angles which was to be formalised for sporting records and consistency towards the end of the later part of the 1900s. These had originally been built as a commercial enterprise which made it into a paying spectator sport.

1920 Kids bikes were produced mainly with three wheels and no chains.

Around this time the cycle was introduced to commerce and postmen and delivery men, tinkers and knife sharpeners etc. could venture further distances, to the outskirts of the towns and villages and even into the countryside. The need to depend on horses was reduced and this cut the costs of grooming, feeding and stabling. Family trips to the countryside with some of the bikes pulling trailers was not uncommon.

1956 By this time the kid's bike had become a necessity and was changed dramatically with the introduction of the BMX and then mountain bikes which were developed in 1970 and first mass produced in 1981. During this time the folding commuter bike was marketed.

1979 Saw the record for a human powered vehicle (HPV) reach over 50mph (81.8kph).

1984 heralded the first world unicycle convention.

1988 The women were included in the Olympic Games.

Other recreations instead of or as well as cycling were ice skating and roller skating where one could pay to go into an indoor arena like a ballroom.

Do I need to say that these activities were also considered beneficial to your health? I will close by listing some of the perceived benefits:

Increased cardiovascular fitness.

Increased muscle strength and flexibility.

Improved joint mobility.

Decreased stress levels.

Improved posture and coordination.

Strengthened bones.

Decreased body fat levels.

Prevention or management of disease.

There you go and I thought I had already written about medicine.

Baby Carriages - Evolution. In the beginning of the century these really were Victorian carriages and they were very posh and large enough to bear the child even after it had started to walk short distances. Every mother wanted the best for their child but also bore in mind that the one purchase would probably have to do for all the rest of the children. Generally most families had neither the space nor the money for indulging in changes as each new born came along.

Things changed in the fifties when early pushchairs became more readily available and affordable to the modern, more affluent, young couples.

The new pushchairs were pushed with the young toddler facing the way they were going and not facing the mother. The chairs were soon to be made to collapse and fold small enough to put into the back of the family car which was by the early 60s becoming almost commonplace.

The people who could not afford these new, relatively expensive, pushchairs could, alternatively, purchase a carrycot which for the younger baby could be used all day and night either indoors, outdoors or in the back seat of the car. We found it a boon as you did not have to wake a sleeping child at the beginning or end of a journey or shopping trip or perhaps indoors, at night, when transferring from the lounge to the bedroom. These and the pushchairs were also very easy to manage on and off of public transport.

The changes from the 70s were mainly in quality and design particularly creating changes so that the new baby had to have the most modern plush style. The social impact was built into the evolution described above.

Trains – Evolution. In 1900 these were the most advanced form of transport and in fact throughout the rest of the century the only real advance was to move from steam to electric and diesel for fuel. I say advancement but in fact it was modification and at the end of the century many people would just as soon travel on the Flying Scotsman as any other train. Tracks and carriages changed little except that an element of comfort was added with better upholstery and perhaps springing. Because of the tracks and gauge running over very rugged terrain, speeds overall, did not actually improve noticeably. The transport of goods, however reduced dramatically as the road transport and roads improved. Roads became king in the same way as the canals had given way to rail.

Trains – Social Impact. The real social impact from the railways actually came about in the Victorian era but as all of these benefits existed at the end of her reign I will run through a list of the key features:

The railways broke down stereotypes and mixed cultures because people from different regions were able to meet.

Political movements spread around the country because members of organisations such as Chartism and the Anti-Corn Law League could travel around the country to drum up support.

Railways became a major employer because people were needed to build, run and maintain them.

British time became standardised because trains had to run to a set timetable across the country.

The government could send soldiers by train to stop political unrest and patrol protests.

The transport of heavy materials became much cheaper.

Railways encouraged people to travel further and this meant people could move to different areas to find work.

MPs were able to travel more quickly between their constituencies and the Houses of Parliament in London.

Perishable food could be moved quickly, so foods such as vegetables and dairy products could now reach the market while they were still fresh.

People were able to take short holidays and day trips.

Political newspapers, pamphlets and newsletters could be delivered by train.

National newspapers could now be delivered locally by early morning.

More people were able to add fish to their diet because ports could transport fresh seafood to markets.

Many sports became regulated because national competitions could be set up for rugby, football and cricket.

Regional products now became household names around the country.

People were willing to invest in railway stocks and this boosted Britain's economy.

One of Britain's biggest exports was locomotives and train parts.

Overall the trains were not run terribly efficiently and did not improve either service or quality to any significant degree throughout the whole of the century. The government got involved in the early sixties when Dr Beeching directed that many cross country hub lines should be closed and out-of-town stations had to be closed. In the south of England this was a time of growing affluence and new housing estates were being developed as far as thirty or forty miles from the centre of London and being sold to commuters. This has never been seen by me as a wise action and where I lived in Crowborough we were to be cut off completely (a new house and no way to get to work). We managed to get a reprieve but the rest of the line was closed and apart from the inconvenience this also cut off the alternative line to Brighton which could operate via Lewes in cases of emergencies, which were not infrequent. By the 1990s the railways were nationalised and speed and comfort improved but as all the twelve coach platforms had been reduced to eight coach lengths after the Beeching cuts, which had predicted the demise of rail services, the expansion of jobs in London and a surge in commuting resulted in more passengers than spaces, causing more not less congestion and more late arrivals. There are proposals for a high speed railway to the north of England but as this proposes out-of-town stations I think it will prove to be only viable for freight and even then the transfer for onward distribution might prove this overly ambitious and ridiculously costly.

Cars and Lorries - Evolution. This is a very different story. In 1900 if you were lucky enough to have a car you probably also needed at least a valet to walk in front with a red flag and probably a chauffeur to do the driving. Firstly human nature says that with the opportunity to be adventurous and travel at speed this would be a major challenge and proved to be so for Malcolm Campbell. In 1933 at the Brighton Trials he travelled along Madeira Drive, Brighton, England, in a straight mile speed of around 130 mph. My elder brother had a poster of his car, the Bluebird, on the wall of his bedroom in the late 1940s to show his appreciation of this machine with its lovely lines in a beautiful blue finish. I think this could have started my love of the motor car. Cars also however became a way of life in the latter part of the century and in the 1990s there was probably at least one car for each household in the U K. Cars were also about the development of the petrol and diesel engines which in the early years powered buses and lorries. The buses themselves replaced the horse drawn trams which were common in the major towns and cities. At the same time the canal boats which were also pulled by horses were fitted with internal combustion engines which meant that they could travel further distances at greater speeds and more conveniently. However due to the environment a canal barge was rarely allowed to travel much over 4 mph.

I did say that trains gave way to lorries but in fact they worked alongside each other to create the first kind of container transport using goods yards to transfer containers from cars to goods trains and vice versa to improve long distance movement of goods

Aerodynamics became more important than overall looks and eventually most cars had very similar lines. This did actually make all travel cheaper but I am not sure how much was added to the purchase price to compensate for research and development. Wind tunnels, before computers, provided the ideal airflows and the research for lighter and stronger metals provided more speed and greater economy.

Coaches – Evolution. Coaches, which in my youth were known as charabancs provided the chance for thirty or forty people to travel together for a day out to the seaside or to and from a holiday in places like Devon and Cornwall as well as the Lake District. Having said that even in the mid-fifties my scout group still took us all the way to Devon on the back of a lorry with all of our gear which we used as seating.

Cars and Lorries and Coaches – Social Impact. In the first half of the century the automobile (car) had little social impact as it was unaffordable to the vast majority of the population. In general the coach provided similar opportunities for travel either at the weekend or for an annual holiday as the train but gave a wider choice of locations. Coaches could also drop you off nearer to your final destination, therefore avoiding the need to transfer to taxis or buses for the final bit of the journey. For this period the lorries changed the commercial scene and became mechanical workhorses. The local use of the shire horses by the local councils and the breweries had not been phased out at the beginning of the Second World War and milk and bread was delivered by a lighter weight horse and cart.

It was after the war that the major events took place to improve transport. Tunnels were built under rivers and ferries were set up to carry cars, lorries and passengers. The two examples I think of are The Dartford Tunnel and Mersey Ferry but there were many more up and down the country with regal names like Queens ferry. Road networks were set up and after major 'A' roads had been improved the first Motorway was built, opened in November 1959, from London (Watford) to Rugby. The 1950s saw wages going up and the cost of utility cars coming down. In 1953 Ford launched the Ford Popular model at a cost of under £500 including taxes. A first level bank manager could expect to earn a little under £1000 p a. and labourers with overtime would have been better off. From the mid to late 60s the car became a must have and boys starting work would hope to buy a cheap second hand car for under £100. Beer was still cheap and there were no drink drive laws so courting couples would go out to country pubs for evening entertainment. With a car it was also easier to have late night parties and visits and not have to try and find the money for a taxi. If you were the one with the car it was common practice for the passengers to club together to cover the cost of the petrol. It was also around this time that hitch-hiking was popular and motorists would stop to give strangers lifts and drop them off near their destination or at a convenient place where they could cadge another ride. Cars could also tow caravans and this became so popular that other motorists started to avoid Cornwall, Devon and Wales because of the lines of slow traffic these caused.

Further expansion of the export business meant that the ports to the continent became overused and the Government agreed with France to build a tunnel under the Channel from

Dover (Folkstone) to Calais. This was originally looked at as a commercial benefit but by providing a separate passenger line, cars and coaches were able to be taken to the continent on a roll-on, roll-off basis. This complemented the holiday flights that were now, dare I say, taking off. Not mentioned above was that trains were the form of transport through the channel tunnel and created a link with the continent to provide direct services first to Paris but later Lille and Brussels and then more southerly destinations.

Ships - Evolution. These were mainly for transport but it was not long before they became essential for early intercontinental travel. This was for business and pleasure (including emigration). Not as in some previous eras, for deportation mainly to Australasia and America. The first real passenger ships to ply between England and America were in the late 1800s and the various shipbuilders and shipping lines soon started competing for the 'Blue Riband' trophy for fastest crossing in either direction, east or west.

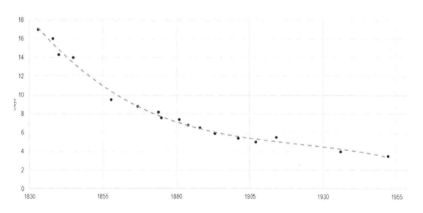

Liner Transatlantic Crossing Times, 1833 – 1952 (in days)

These ships were carrying several hundred first class and second class passengers and over a thousand in third and steerage.

In simple terms Liners were destined to become obsolete with the development of airplanes but as we see later this was by no means the whole story.

International shipping was very important but coastal and tramp ships were used in abundance moving large quantities of things like coal and steel and obviously supporting the fishing industry. Before road transport took off these ships were only competing with canals and trains and in many coastal areas particularly they could move more and move it quicker. The fishing industry still needs fishing boats but in general all other ships from tiny pleasure craft to massive cruisers are now part of the leisure industry which I will handle in the next part of transport.

Ships – Social Impact. Shipping changed dramatically in two ways in the 1960s. Commercially affecting goods and services, and socially with the introduction of purpose built cruise liners.

It's difficult to believe now, but until the 1970s virtually all goods were shipped around the world loose, that is, crammed into the holds of old fashioned cargo ships. While several people had toyed with the idea of putting cargo in big boxes, trucking company owner Malcolm McLean is generally credited with inventing the shipping container.

McClean bought an old oil tanker in the mid-1950s and began experimenting with it as a vehicle to carry trucks. When that idea didn't work out, he switched his focus to boxes. By 1965 the world bulk carrier fleet exceeded one thousand vessels, more than double the number seen five years earlier. Then a further change came in around 1968 when container sizes had been standardised and ships began to be purpose made. Container ships did away with weeks of warehousing and re-packaging and the demand for labour that once existed in port cities diminished very, very significantly, it is probably the biggest change and dislocation that has occurred at any time in the ports globally.

With the increased facilities for travel and with the trains, coaches and planes providing new-fangled package holidays both at home and abroad it was the obvious outcome that the inter-continental liners be re-utilised as cruise liners to travel the Mediterranean and the Caribbean. This was so successful that it also soon followed the container ships and they were purpose building cruise liners. By the end of the 1900s ships carried well over 3000 passengers who had swimming pools, restaurants, tanning parlours, bowling alleys and shopping malls as well as sun loungers and bars.

The end product of these changes provided the general public with the benefits of fresher foods, cheaper goods and more affordable travel facilities.

Aircraft - Evolution. The early aircraft developed around 1900 but the thought was there earlier. Here is a timeline with comments:

1000 BC – First kites are invented in China.

852 BC – The English King Bladud is apparently killed attempting to fly.

1485–1500 – Leonardo da Vinci designs flying machines.

1709 – Model glider design.

1783 – The first untethered manned hot air balloon flight was on 21 November 1783 in Paris, France in a balloon created by the Montgolfier brothers.

1903 – First powered flight. Orville and Wilbur Wright make the first recorded powered, sustained and controlled flight in a heavier-than-air flying machine.

1904 – Richard Pearse from New Zealand makes his first recorded powered flight of more than a few seconds, though witnesses contend his first flight may have been just before the Wright brothers.

1906 – Alberto Santos-Dumont makes the first successful powered flight in Europe.

1911 – Kiwi aviator George Bolt's flying career began in the South Island in 1911. Aged just 18, he launched a glider that he had designed and built himself from the Cashmere Hills above Christchurch. In 1911 Bolt took New Zealand's first aerial photographs. In 1916 he began work as an apprentice mechanic at the Walsh brothers' New Zealand Flying School in Auckland.

1927 – Charles Lindbergh completes the first solo non-stop trans-Atlantic flight.

1930 – Jet engine invented. British inventor Frank Whittle invents the jet engine.

1932 – Amelia Earhart is the first woman to fly a solo non-stop trans-Atlantic flight.

1932–1937 – Record-breaking flights

1939 – First jet-propelled aircraft. Germany's Heinkel 178 is the first fully jet-propelled aircraft to fly.

1940s – Aerial agriculture, seed sowing, top dressing and crop dusting are developed in New Zealand with ex-WW2 pilots and planes.

1947 – Charles Yeager pilots the first aircraft to exceed the speed of sound in level flight.

1969 – First supersonic transport flight. First flights of supersonic transport – Soviet TU-144 and Anglo-French Concorde.

1976 – Concorde begins its first passenger-carrying service. The turbojet-powered supersonic passenger jet airliner operated until 2003. Concorde had a maximum speed more than twice the speed of sound.

1979 – Longest human-powered flight. Bryan Allen pedals the Gossamer Albatross across the English Channel, breaking the distance record for human-powered flight.

1986 – Dick Rutan and Jeana Yeager fly the US ultralight Voyager around the world in a 9-day non-stop flight from California to California

People are always seeking to beat each other and as you can see in aviation the competition gave rise to rapid advancement in speed, design and invention. When we look at space travel this progress might actually appear sluggish.

Percival Elliott Fansler, a Florida sales representative for a manufacturer of diesel engines for boats, became fascinated with Benoist's progress in designing aircraft that could take off and land in the water. The two men started corresponding, and eventually Fansler proposed "a real commercial line from somewhere to somewhere else." He proposed that the airline fly between St. Petersburg and Tampa.

In 1913, a trip between the two cities, sitting on opposite sides of Tampa Bay, took two hours by steamship or from 4 to 12 hours by rail. Traveling by automobile around the bay took about 20 hours. A flight would take about 20 minutes.

1914, the world's first scheduled passenger airline service took off, operating between St. Petersburg and Tampa, Fla. The St. Petersburg-Tampa Airboat Line was a short-lived endeavour — only four months — but it paved the way for today's daily transcontinental flights.

The first flight's pilot was Tony Jannus

Jannus already a popular figure in aviation gave flying exhibitions, tested military planes, and flew long-distance airplanes and airboats. He piloted the first tests of airborne machine guns. On March 1, 1912, he carried Capt. Albert Berry aloft to make the first parachute jump from an airplane.

Aircraft changed both public life and warfare but by the end of the 1900s all this was taken for granted and so many people wanted to travel for business or pleasure that expanding airports and ensuring quicker access and regress seemed the most important task in hand. I think it was felt that the size of planes which usually carried several hundred passengers had progressed far enough.

Aircraft – Social Impact. This brought the same benefits globally as trains had nationally; faster more efficient transport of goods and services and people (both business and pleasure). Holidays became more exotic and package tours organised by the likes of Thomas Cook were developed for the larger population.

The popularity of air travel meant that it was not only governments putting money into the industry to develop military aircraft but this development gave the industry the opportunity to improve passenger travel to the extent Boeing built a plane with a lounge-bar on an upper deck for first class travellers.

Rockets – Evolution and Social Impact. Rockets were the introduction to spacecraft and in my teenage years we heard that a dog was going to be sent up in an orbital spacecraft as a forerunner to sending people into space. They even suggested that people might walk on the moon. Here is my short history timeline.

R-7	1957	First intercontinental Ballistic Missile (ICBM) developed.	USSR
Sputnik 1	1957	First artificial satellite.	USSR
Sputnik 2	1957	First animal (dog named Laika) sent to the orbit.	USSR
Explorer 6	1959	First photograph of Earth taken from the orbit (by NASA).	USA
Vostok I	1961	First manned flight carrying Yuri Gagarin	USSR
OSO-1	1962	First orbital solar observatory (by NASA).	USA
Vostok 6	1963	First woman in space (Valentina Tereshkova).	USSR
Luna 10	1966	First artificial satellite around the Moon.	USSR
Apollo 8	1968	First piloted orbital mission of Moon (by NASA).	USA
Apollo 11	1969	First human on the Moon and first space launch from a celestial body (by NASA) - Commander Neil Armstrong and Pilot Buzz Aldrin.	USA
Luna 16	1970	First automatic sample return from the Moon.	USSR
Salyut 1	1971	First space station.	USSR
Pioneer 10	1972	First human made object that had been sent on escape trajectory away from the Sun (by NASA).	USA
Mariner 10	1974	First photograph of Venus from Space (by NASA).	USA
Venera 13	1982	First Venus soil samples and sound recording of another world.	USSR
STS-41-B	1984	First untethered spacewalk, Bruce McCandless II (by NASA).	USA
Voyager 1	1990	First photograph of the whole Solar System (by NASA).	USA

I am sure that this table means more to some people than others and although I can remember a lot of things the progression through the many Apollo and Voyager et al missions is definitely not one of them.

What I do remember is the, dare I say thrill, of watching one of the capsules returning from outer space which looked like an oversized beach ball landing in the sea and then seeing two fully grown men in spacesuits clamber out.

Later we were to see pictures sent directly from the moon and observe the first man on the moon. Even today I find these escapades almost unbelievable and there are still sceptics that think the whole thing was done in a hidden film studio. No, to my mind this is just one of the many mind blowing advancements of the century and is one of the reasons why I am trying to bring to light how the 1900s progressed in my eyes. With rockets there was very little real social impact to affect day-to-day life.

CHAPTER FIVE

TECHNOLOGY

Materials. The advancement of technology depended on the advancement in the first place of the science applied to creating new materials and then later to some of these being miniaturised. The development links are not all obvious and are often interrelated, for instance the computer which was about 5ft high 6ft long and 4ft wide after the war, at the end of the century was a very small laptop. This had evolved from metal rings by electric wires being magnetised through to miniaturised silicon chips. To get to this state most modern materials were used from metal (for magnetic rings), wire (to carry electric current), quartz (for accurate timing), Silicon (for semi conduction and electronic circuitry)and beside these what I can only describe as non-materials are radio waves and radar which enabled the movement of sound and vision through thin air.

Around the mid-century it was discovered how to split the atom and atom bombs and nuclear weapons were developed for defence and as a deterrent. Nuclear power stations provided electricity but before this Bakelite was often used to encase radios and then plastic/polystyrene took over.

I will now try to provide the evolution of different technologies and try not to repeat myself too often.

Telephones – Evolution. In my history I will go back to the 1800s in order to put the beginning of the 20th century into perspective.

1878 Bell demonstrated the telephone to Queen Victoria on 14th January at Osborne House.

1886 In this year 50 million telegrams were sent compared with 33 million the previous year.

1891 The first submarine telephone cable was laid between England and France enabling telephone conversations to be made between London and Paris.

1895 The Post Office trunk telephone system was opened to the public on 16th July. 78,839,600 telegrams dealt with in the UK.

1898 First long distance cable laid between London to Birmingham was started in 1897 and finished in this year. The cable was mainly used for telegraph traffic, but was also used experimentally for telephony.

1899 A Telegraph Act was passed in this year to enable local municipalities outside London to set up their own local telephone systems. Later in the year the Post Office began laying an extensive system of telephone lines in London.

The policy of municipal telephony in provincial towns would have seemed a natural development in adding to the already wide powers of local authorities in providing gas, water, electricity, transport and other public amenities. In the event, it was to prove a failure. Only six actually opened telephone systems and only the service provided by Hull continues to the end of the century. The remaining five services were all sold to the National Telephone Company or to the Post Office by the end of 1913.

1900 The first Central Battery exchange in Europe was opened in Telephone Avenue, Bristol. This development was of great benefit to individual telephone subscribers. In the Central Battery System the whole energy required for signalling and speaking was drawn from one large battery at the exchange. The subscribers' magneto generator and primary battery were consequently no longer needed.

1901 The first municipal telephone exchange was inaugurated in Glasgow on 28th March and Tunbridge Wells followed in June.

On 12th December, Marconi, transmitted the first radio signals across the Atlantic Ocean.

1902 The first Post Office exchange in London was opened on 1st March 'Central Exchange' with a capacity for 14,000 subscribers. 'City' Exchange was the second (capacity 18,000) followed by 'Mayfair' to serve the West End, 'Western' for Kensington and 'Victoria' for Westminster in the same year. Several other Post Office exchanges were also opened in the London suburbs.

A licence to operate a local telephone service was granted to Hull Corporation for the first time on 8th August.

1903 A cheap rate telephone service was introduced by the Post Office; six minutes were allowed for the normal price of a three-minute call between 8 pm and 6 am.

1904 The first municipal telephone exchange in Hull was opened on 28 November.

1906 The Post Office's first coin-operated call box was installed at Ludgate Circus, London.

1907 Lee de Forest (1873-1961) added a third element to Fleming's thermionic valve (the diode) to create a triode. This had the ability to amplify faint signals, making possible long distance radio and even television communications. The triode was a remarkable invention and was only matched in importance by the invention of the transistor which replaced it some 40 years later.

Charles L Krumm and his son, H Krumm, introduced the first stop-start type of telegraph. This instrument, known as the 'Teletype', used a typewriter keyboard for direct sending and a five unit code with stop-start signals, as used by later teleprinters.

1908 The Post Office opened its first ship-to-shore wireless radio coast station at Bolt Head, Devon and further licensed stations were soon added.

1910 A trunk telephone cable was opened between Manchester and Liverpool and The National Telephone Company was licensed on 10th August to provide fire, police and ambulance telephone circuits.

1912 On 1st January the Postmaster-General took over the system of the National Telephone Company at a cost of £12,515,264, inheriting 9,000 employees, 1,500,000 miles of wire and 1,565 exchanges - of which 231 had more than 300 subscribers each. The National Telephone Company provided for 561,738 subscribers altogether. Just under 70 exchanges were of the Central Battery type; most of the rest were of the magneto type.

For the first time a unified telephone system was available throughout most of Britain. No fewer than 450 new exchanges were opened in places where there had previously been no telephone service. The first experimental public automatic telephone exchange installed in the UK was opened for service at Epsom, Surrey, on 18th May.

The SS Titanic sank with great loss of life on 15th April after hitting an iceberg. But 700 passengers who would otherwise have been lost were saved as a result of a distress call by wireless telegraphy.

Wooden telephone kiosks introduced.

1914 A submarine telephone cable was laid between Dover and Dunkirk. Telephone service opened with Switzerland. The third automatic telephone exchange in this country was opened at Hereford on 1st August and had a 500line capacity.

1918 Leeds automatic telephone exchange was opened with an ultimate capacity of 15,000, and the first exchange in this country capable of being extended to give service to 100,000 subscribers. It was also the first in which the caller was required to dial five figures for every local call.

Further exchanges were opened throughout the country. The Wireless Telegraphy Board, the beginnings of the frequency management structure that exists today was set up.

1920 Private Automatic Branch Exchanges (PABXs) were introduced. These later became the system that most companies used for 'in house' switchboards.

A telephone conversation by wireless radio was exchanged from a private residence in London to an aeroplane in flight to Paris. The Post Office also commenced its long-distance radio-telegraph service to ships.

1921 Concrete telephone kiosks introduced.

The first Rural Automatic Exchange (RAX), a 40-line facility was brought into service. Rural areas were until now served by small manual exchanges attended by caretaker operators. Exchanges with fewer than 20 subscribers did not normally give service at night or on Sundays.

1922 The first automatic exchange in Hull was opened.

First Teleprinter trials.

1923 London Toll system extended to Brighton and Aylesbury.

1924 The Telephone No. 150 was introduced, it was innovatory in introducing the dial to most subscribers for the first time

A modern red telephone kiosk (K2) was designed and approved.

1925 A new type of coin-box was introduced, the well-known Button A and Button B prepayment equipment, and for over 25 years its design remained unchanged despite various developments in the design of kiosks.

1927 An international time signal was broadcast throughout the world from Rugby Radio Station. A joint development with the Admiralty and Board of Trade, it was intended to assist mariners. The time signals were generated from the Royal Greenwich Observatory.

1928 New York telephone basic rate reduced to £9 for 3 minutes conversation (this sounds like a fortune in 1928, probably 2 weeks wages or more).

London Toll Area extended throughout a lot of the south of England.

As of March 31st the UK had:-

Telephone Kiosks   23,998

Telephone Exchanges - Manual   4,206

Telephone Exchanges - Automatic   111

Telephone Calls - Inland   1,070,500,000

Telephone Calls - Trunks   102,206,596

Telephone Calls - Overseas   702,000

1929. An audio conferencing 'conference communication' system composed of transmitters and loudspeakers was used on 23rd October to connect audiences in Manchester, Liverpool, Birmingham, Glasgow, Leeds, Newcastle, Cardiff, Southampton and Portsmouth with the Institution of Electrical Engineers in London.

22 experimental police telephone boxes, installed as part of a new scheme for policing were made available for general use. The Post Office adopts the Teleprinter as the standard instrument for inland telegraph circuits.

1930 A picture telegraph (facsimile) service between the Central Telegraph Office and some European cities were opened.

A radio-telephone service was opened with Australia, Africa and Argentina

A motor cycle telegraph messages service was inaugurated at Bournemouth.

1931 The first 200-line unit automatic exchange (No. 6) was opened.

1932 The first ultra-short-wave radio telephone link, used as part of the inland telephone network, was set up across the Bristol Channel, over a distance of 13 miles.

The first large centralised Directory Enquiry Bureau was opened in August.

A standard switchboard was introduced for police telephone and signal systems.

1933 Telephone service was opened with India, Northern and Southern Rhodesia and Turkey.

1934 The transferred-charge service was first introduced on the inland telephone system. This enabled callers to have a call made through an operator charged to the person receiving that call. (This was, in my youth, used by boys after a night out and with no money left to call home for dad to arrange transport. A magnificent idea until dad refused to take the charge.)

The first 800-line Unit Automatic Exchange (UAX 7) was introduced. Still not very large but a big increase from the early 100 line units.

1936 The speaking clock was introduced, a service at first available only in London The Post Office had held a competition to decide on the voice to be recorded, and subscribers dialling TIM would hear the 'golden voice' of Miss Jane Cain, a London telephone operator, giving the Greenwich Time correct to one-tenth of a second. The voice of Jane Cain was replaced by that of Pat Simmons in 1963.

1937 The 999 emergency telephone service was made available throughout the country. When 999 was dialled a buzzer sounded in the exchange and a red light flashed to draw an operator's immediate attention.

1938 As of March 31st the UK had:-

Telephones Stations   3,050,012

Telephone Kiosks   48,168

Telephone Exchanges - Manual   3,104

Telephone Exchanges - Automatic   2,559

Telephone Calls - Inland   2,059,300,000

Telephone Calls - Trunks   105,838,286

Telephone Calls - Overseas   1,887,000

1939 During the first six months of the war, before heavy German bombing started, the Post Office made use of the opportunity to complete the link up by telephone and telegraph of Home Defences, particularly Fighter and Anti-Aircraft Commands. By the time of the Battle of Britain the Headquarters of Fighter Command was a communications centre in touch with all defence stations and information sources across the country via Post Office facilities. From here the Commander-in-Chief was able to observe the broad 'air picture' and co-ordinate his Fighter Groups. Additionally a complex teleprinter network was also installed. With the collapse of France and when invasion seemed a real possibility, new aerodromes, battery sites, searchlight centres and radar stations had to be set up - and all needed linking with telephone communications, again carried out by Post Office engineers. Later in the war, as part of the preparations for the Normandy invasion, a new network of cables, switchboards, telephones and teleprinters had to be set up along England's south coast to control the D-Day build up. Once the invasion was under-way, new cross-channel cables were laid and by VE-Day the Post Office had made direct communication possible by telephone or teleprinter to all Allied Forces in North West Europe.

On the home front the Post Office had soon organised itself to meet the demands of the war. ARP services were set up in all departments, and a Home Guard Force of over 50,000 was raised to defend Post Office telegraph and telephone systems in the event of invasion. Other Post Office Defence Forces

114

included medical staff, fire fighters and first aiders, all of whom were particularly called upon during the bombing raids of the early war years. During this time Post Office engineers battled to repair bomb damage to plant and cables, yet were still able to open the additional military channels of communication described above. This you should recognise was not a nationalised industry at this time and my guess is it was not overly unionised.

Even with all the British Bulldog attitude I doubt this kind of commitment would have been forthcoming in a similar way in 1999.

1942 Shared service was introduced on automatic exchanges. I think this was what I knew as a party line where two subscribers used a single line and if someone was talking when you picked up the phone politeness said you put it down and try later. Trying to hold your breath and listen in was not the done thing.

1943 Subscriber dialling in London Director Area was extended.

In March the long wave building ("C" Building) at Rugby Radio Station was severely damaged by fire. A newly built counterpart to GBR was able to take traffic within a few days. The damage to the building and GBR was repaired within six months.(Again could we have achieved this at the end of the century.)

1945 The basic rate for a London-New York call was £3 for three minutes' conversation.

1947 Cable & Wireless Ltd. was nationalised on 1st January by the Treasury's purchase of the company's shares, and by the Post Office's acquisition of the company's telecommunications assets in Britain.

1948 A shared service was made obligatory for all new residential applicants. As of March 31st the UK had:-

Telephones Stations   4,652,704

Telephone Kiosks   52,098

Telephone Exchanges - Manual   2,197

Telephone Exchanges - Automatic   3,840

Telephone Calls - Inland   2,681,000,000

Telephone Calls - Trunks   216,614,671

Telephone Calls - Overseas   1,702,600

1949 quartz clocks provided by the Post Office replaced the mechanical pendulum clocks in the Greenwich Time Signal (GTS) generating apparatus at the Royal Observatory.

The radio-telephone service with ships in the Thames Estuary was introduced.

1955 In 1959 the first versions of the new Pay-on-Answer payphones were being introduced and at the end of the 1950s began to supersede the 'Button A and B' models. This was made necessary following the introduction of Subscriber Trunk Dialling (STD) in major towns. The Subscriber Trunk

Dialling (STD) service, whereby telephone callers are able to make trunk calls automatically without the aid of the operator, was introduced into the United Kingdom by the Queen dialling a call on 5th December 1958 from Bristol Central Telephone Exchange to the Lord Provost of Edinburgh, over 300 miles away - the greatest distance over which a subscriber trunk call could be made at the time. Afterwards, the Queen operated a switch which put 18,000 telephones connected to Bristol Central onto the new system.

1959 A car radiophone service for vehicle users was introduced in South Lancashire.

1960 The first London STD exchange (Watford) was opened.

1961 A radio telephone service from aircraft was introduced

1962 International subscriber dialling of Telex calls introduced.

1963 International Subscriber Trunk Dialling (ISD) was introduced, allowing London subscribers to dial Paris numbers.

1967 The Quartz TIM clocks were replaced as caesium atomic standards were introduced. However in 1999 Rugby still transmits the Greenwich Time Signal, which is derived from the National Physical Laboratory's atomic resonance standard. The laboratory is now the UK's national centre for time - its atomic clocks generate the UK's time standard, which is made available via transmissions from Rugby Radio Station.

1969 A second aerial at the Post Office Satellite Communications Station, Goonhilly Downs, was completed.

The station could now communicate simultaneously with satellites over the Atlantic and Indian Oceans. In July, Goonhilly was the European terminal for the television coverage of Man's first steps on the moon at the time of the Apollo 11 moon landing.

1970 The International Subscriber Trunk Dialling service was extended to allow London subscribers to dial New York numbers - the world's first major Inter-Continental subscriber dialling service. The cost was 10s (50p) per minute. Compare this with the £9 for three minutes in the twenties.

Gardening and Bedtime Story Services were introduced as an addition to the range of recorded information services provided by Post Office Telecommunications.

1972 The ten millionth telephone exchange line was installed in the United Kingdom.

1975 20 Millionth telephone installed by January.

1979 The STD system, commenced in 1958, was completed to allow direct dialling between all UK subscribers.

1981 British Telecom offered telephones for sale for the first time as an alternative to rental. Eleven phoneshops were opened in major department stores.

The first cashless, card-operated payphone - the Cardphone - was introduced as a new service.

Radiopaging was extended to give a virtually nationwide service.

Britain's first automatic carphone service, System 4, was launched in London on 14th July, whereby customers were able to make direct calls without having to go through an operator

1982 IDD (International Direct Dialling) was made available throughout the United Kingdom.

Telemessages (overnight delivery services) superseded the inland telegram service on 30 September, which meant the demise of the telegraph boy on either a bike or a motor cycle. Very sad for the nostalgic but it removed the fear of receiving bad news which throughout the war came by telegram or with a policeman knocking on the door.

1983 The transatlantic submarine cable, TAT 7, laid the previous year, was officially inaugurated on 16 September.

British Telecom's first satellite coast station came into service with the opening of a new dish aerial at Goonhilly. Telephone and telex calls could be made or received direct for the first time to almost anywhere in the world, via Britain.

British Telecom offered car telephone radio sets for the first time.

Display Page, British Telecom's radiopager with a digital message display, was launched. A ten-digit liquid crystal display on the new pager could be used to identify the caller (by giving a phone number), or to convey a message.

Confertel, a new flexible and inexpensive means of holding meetings by telephone, was introduced.

1984 The first UK, and the world's largest, digital international telephone exchange was opened. The new exchange provided an extra 13,800 lines, and could handle up to 144,000 call attempts an hour.

The search for a new voice for the speaking clock ended on 5 December when Brian Cobby, an assistant supervisor in a telephone exchange at Withdean, Brighton, was selected.

Trainphone introduced on BR Western Region. London - Swansea route.

1985 The new speaking clock was inaugurated at 11 o'clock on 2nd April when the voice of Brian Cobby replaced that of Pat Simmons, the voice of the clock for the previous 22 years. The new clock was digital and, with no moving parts, more reliable and accurate than the old equipment.

The first UK operational undersea optical fibre cable was laid, linking the Isle of Wight to the mainland across the Solent.

The UK's public payphone system had not been amongst the most efficient in the world, but when a programme of change was completed in 1988 the Quality of Service report showed a 96 per cent reliability. This success rate continued, compared to only 72 per cent in 1987. As a result of the programme, there were 80,000 of the stainless steel design kiosks in service by 1996, in addition to 30,000 hooded/canopied phones in locations such as railway stations or shopping centres and 15,000 old style red boxes in heritage sites.

The Message Master radiopager was launched. It was the first pager with a mini screen for written messages.

1986 The first international optical fibre undersea link between the United Kingdom and Belgium was opened.

The world's first all-digital international public telephone service was opened between gateways in London and Tokyo.

1987 Electronic Yellow Pages was launched.

The world's first instantaneous translation of speech by a computer was demonstrated by British Telecom's Research Laboratories.

1988 An optical fibre undersea link to the Isle of Man - the longest unregenerated system in Europe - was inaugurated on 28th March. The following year, the equivalent of 25,000 simultaneous telephone conversations was carried over a single optical fibre link in the optical submarine cable.

1989 The world's first satellite telephone communications system for airline passengers, Skyphone, had its commercial debut on a British Airways 747 in February.

BT Marine, British Telecom's undersea cable laying subsidiary, announced in November the building of a new 12,500 tonne cableship to replace the CS Alert in 1991, to be called CS Sovereign. The new ship was launched in 1991.

1990 The 100 millionth BT Phonecard was produced.

The biggest change to the London telephone numbering system since the introduction of All Figure Numbering took place on 6th May with the code change from 01 to 071 for inner London and 081 for outer London.

British Telecom had publicised the code changes over the previous year through television, radio, newspapers, poster sites, mailings and so forth. A code change party at Telecom Tower attended by several celebrities marked the actual changeover itself, which was broadcast live on television. To further celebrate the occasion British Telecom donated £1 million to the Royal Academy of Dramatic Art towards its new premises in central London.

There was a further code change in 1995.

1991

On 30th May a new BT cableship was launched in Rotterdam named CS Sovereign, the first new wholly owned cableship for 15 years. She was built by the Dutch firm, Van der Giessen-de Noord, who won the £32 million contract after international competitive tendering. CS Sovereign handled repair and maintenance to fibre optic systems and intended to replace CS Alert.

1992 The 100,000th BT payphone was installed at Dunsop Bridge near Clitheroe in Lancashire. The site was chosen as being the village nearest to the centre of Great Britain.

1994 Directory enquiry charges for UK telephone numbers were reduced from 45p to 25p per enquiry on 1 September.

Free fully itemised telephone bills were made available to residential customers to cover every single call.

Call Return and Caller Display were launched on 22 November as part of the portfolio of Select Services available to UK customers connected to digital exchanges.

Callers could prevent their numbers being forwarded by dialling "141" before the number they were calling.

1995 Oftel (government telephone quango) nominated 16th April as National Code Change day, Phoneday. The code change effectively gave every geographic number an extra "1" after the "0". Leeds, Bristol, Sheffield, Nottingham and Leicester were given new codes and new numbers were introduced to cater for future growth. The international code for calls from the UK changed from "010" to "00".

The UK network became totally digital on 11th March 1998 with the closure of the last electronic exchanges.

1996 Research for BT Payphones revealed widespread appreciation of the availability, maintenance and reliability of the existing payphones and the standards to which they were maintained. Despite liking certain features of the stainless steel designs introduced from the 1980s, such as the fact that they were lighter, more airy and more accessible for people with disabilities than the traditional style, customers felt that there was still room for improvement. Popular opinion was that the square shape seemed clinical and that something softer and more rounded would be preferable. The colour of the phonebox itself, particularly the roof, had to satisfy a number of requirements, in particular it had to be practical to keep clean and bright enough for customers with visual impairments. After a number of experiments, red proved to be the colour that best met the required criteria, with the added advantage that it reflected something of the character of the traditional red K6 kiosk designed by Sir Giles Gilbert Scott in the 1930s.

The new design resulted from collaboration between GKN, who manufactured the existing style of payphone, and the design agency DCA. It was also extremely cost effective to produce, as it used the same basic carcass as the existing payphone housing.

The first of the new look phone boxes appeared on the streets in the early autumn, with approximately 5,000 installed over the next year.

Compare this to the war effort which had decisions and results without all of the hassle of consultations and with a perfectly satisfactory outcome.

1997 A new information service allowed details of both the calling number and the address from which a 999 call had been made to be transferred automatically to the emergency authority operator's screen.

1999, BT operated a network of over 140,000 public payphones of various designs across the UK, compared to 81,000 ten years previously, with an average of 5,000 new units being installed each year.

Telephone – Social Impact. The evolution above has stayed with the telephone landline which by the turn of the century (1990s) seemed to be going to replace traditional cables with fibre optics and to proceed to expand broadband speed and coverage. Mobile phones grew out of the radio pager and satellite technology and look to be incorporating broadband and television into the one instrument in the near future, but I will address this development as part of the evolution of computers.

So, going back to the beginning of the 1900s, as a social tool the telephone did not exist. The impact and growth was very steady throughout first half of the century as it became more available and then a necessary part of business life and then almost a social requirement. The evolution shows that between 1938 and 1948 the number of telephone stations grew by 50% to four and a half million and trunk calls doubled as manual exchanges were gradually replaced by automatics. The number of kiosks had almost trebled and was still growing. These kiosks were a major part of the social need for family communication and sometimes people would be seen standing outside a phone box waiting for an incoming call. This was because the ordinary individual either could not afford or could not get a landline. It was not until well into the sixties that enough phones started to become available at an economical price and in a reasonable time frame. I was team secretary for a local football team and recently found a copy of the available players' names and addresses. Only about 60% had telephone numbers which were for them or a neighbour, for the rest in case of need it was get on your bike and visit with your team change request.

The first real benefactors of the telephone were the business community. The travelling salesman was still a requirement but at the end of each day or week he could communicate with his boss and plan for the next campaign and order more goods. One benefit was that he did not have to carry a lot of excess stock as he could tailor his order to his sales and therefore mostly only carry samples. In the offices and warehouses business could be carried out with a less extensive messenger service or the slower mail system. With the introduction of the PABX exchange into the business environment the telephonist became almost as important as the senior secretary as she was the first point of contact, however, she could not support the minor requirements of the boss who wanted his bets placed, his money banked and his coffee and sandwiches delivered to his desk among other things.

The second half of the century saw quicker and more significant changes but the impact now was more on business improvement and change rather than streaming the existing activities.

In around 1960 the banks in London introduced a foreign exchange money desk and traded foreign currencies as spot or forward contracts. Ostensibly these were to cover the import and export demands of their customers but it was not long before they found ways of using the telephone and telex facilities to, in effect, gamble and gain better rates for their customers and even gamble on rate fluctuations to make a profit. International calls enabled importers to perhaps add to or cancel and order at short notice where in the past the order would already have been despatched before the necessary mail arrived.

While the telephone exchanges were still not digitalised the old method of hailing a cab was being replaced with minicabs. I think it was Welbeck 4444 that was the first number available in London to book a 'taxi' by phone. The black cab drivers were outraged.

Doctor and dental appointments could be arranged over the phone which was a great improvement on my youth when you walked round to the surgery to join the queue for either the morning or evening surgery. It seemed to me that I was always ill on a Thursday evening when our particular doctor had an evening off. One time when I was very unwell we went round only to find that in the turmoil we had forgotten it was Thursday. The notice on the door said walk to the surgery just over a mile away. When we had been seen we were told to walk home collect some clothes and then walk to the station and travel to a hospital in London for an immediate operation. The doctor had spent a good half an hour arranging the appointment using his phone getting through to various hospitals via the local telephone operator. By the end of the century this could have been – call a cab – doctor – call a cab – home – station – station – black cab to hospital. No several miles walking with severe ear and head ache.

Telephones were a definite boon to society even with negative side effects such as having a betting account and the boss being able to contact you day or night.

Radio - Evolution. Regardless of who created the very first radio, on December 12, 1901, Marconi's place in history was forever sealed when he became the first person to transmit signals across the Atlantic Ocean.

Prior to the 1920s, the radio was primarily used to contact ships that were out at sea. Radio communications were not very clear, so operators typically relied on the use of Morse code messages. This was of great benefit to vessels in the water, particularly during emergency situations. With World War I, the importance of the radio became apparent and its usefulness increased significantly. During the war, the military used it almost exclusively and it became an invaluable tool in sending and receiving messages to the armed forces in real time, without the need for a physical messenger.

In the 1920s, following the war, civilians began to purchase radios for private use. While manufactured radios were finding their way into the mainstream, home-built radio receivers were a solution for some households. In my and my children's schooldays we were taught how to make a crystal set similar to those used by our grandparents.

In Britain, radio broadcasts began in 1922 with the British Broadcasting Company, or BBC, in London. The broadcasts quickly spread across the UK but failed to usurp newspapers until 1926 when the newspapers went on strike. At this point the radio and the BBC became the leading source of information for the public. It also became a source of entertainment in which gathering in front of the radio as a family became a common occurrence in many households. Radio has become much more than Tesla or Marconi could have ever imagined. My neighbours and relatives in London in the Second World War were glued with their ear to the radio waiting for the first notes of Beethoven's Fifth which always introduced an urgent news flash. Traditional radios and radio broadcasting have become a thing of the past. Instead, by the end of the century it had steadily evolved to keep up with the current technology, with satellite and streaming internet stations gaining popularity. Radios became a must have accessory for every new car and was a required added item for other models. In addition to music, radio talk shows became a popular option. Ever since pirate radio transmissions like Radio Luxembourg in the 1950s private radio stations have proliferated particularly on medium wave and FM (frequency modulated) but long and short wave were still in use in the 1990s. On the two-way radios front, newer digital two-way radios allow for one-to-one communication and short-range radios have improved communications at worksites and handheld radios have become essential in sports, television production and even commercial airline operations.

Radio – Social Impact The main impact commercially was the handheld radios as described above but radios made a big difference to some of the day-to-day life. It first brought family life together in the middle of the century but in the early 50s the portable radio, which had quite a small battery, (unlike the liquid acid type that had to be exchanged at the local shop where they were recharged for future exchanges) was taken out to the countryside and the beaches or using top of the market sets used during the actual car journey. Transistor radios became popular with replaceable small batteries and were carried everywhere by teenagers to keep up with Pop-music hit parade both to learn the words and know the current scene. Later radio was everywhere blaring out over loudspeakers in shops and malls and some companies provided background music to staff in appropriate areas. Although Television had made its mark radio was still a must have.

Gramophones – Evolution and Social Impact. As far as the 20th century is concerned the introduction of the 7in flat disc turning at 78 rpm (revs per minute) is where it all began.

Before 1925, all 78s were recorded by means of the artist singing or speaking into a horn, the power of their voice directly vibrating the recording stylus and thus cutting the wax of the master disc. Collectors call these discs "acoustic" recordings.

The sounds to be preserved are directed into a large horn, which at its tapered end is connected to a cutting stylus. In response to the vibrations of air in the horn, the stylus cuts a spiral groove in the thick wax coating of a cylinder or disc, rotated steadily by means of a crank. The cutting process creates variations in the groove analogous to the varying frequency and amplitude of the vibrations; the stylus moves up and down in "hill-and-dale" or "vertical cut" recording and from side to side in "lateral cut" recording.

Recording and playing speeds ranged from 72 to 86 rpm before the standard settled at 78 (though Columbia, for example, issued 80 rpm discs for some time after 1920). The old mechanical wind up gramophone that we got from our grandparents had a speed adjuster that you could alter for each record to obtain what you felt was the expected result. The gramophone itself played by reversing the recording process and sending sound out through a horn. The HMV logo with a dog next to an old fashioned gramophone depicts this very well. By around 1920 lateral cut recording was the norm; a less exacting technique than vertical cut, it produced a level of fidelity adequate to the standard of the equipment the general public could afford to buy.

Electrical recording was first used in 1925. After that 78s were recorded by the artist singing or speaking into a microphone and amplifier which then cut the master record. This allowed a wider range of sound to be recorded. The physical format of electrical recordings remained the same as that of the many acoustical ones utilizing the lateral cut technique. This electrical recording was superseded by the introduction of magnetic tape in 1947 but you still bought 78s on discs.

To play a record you needed, originally a needle and later stylus, to pass over the moving surface. The steel needles were hardwearing but we did, at times, try to sharpen them. The stylus was more expensive but necessary on the modern electric machines and had to be replaced when worn. We could buy different qualities and had to purchase at least 25 at a time.

Although you could buy a portable gramophone they were not used for picnics or beach outings but rather to take to someone's house when they were willing to host a record evening but did not own a record player. On these occasions all the guests took records along (these were carefully labelled to ensure you did not have one purloined).

Gramophones were outdated by tape recorders which apart from playing cassettes were able, in some instances, to allow you to make your own recordings either selfies at home or maybe of your own band or group or pinch something off the radio.

Needless to say that from the sixties onwards technology changed very rapidly and gramophones and tape recorders were soon old hat and electronics took over – more later. At this point before I close on gramophones I will recall for you the words of the comedy duo Flanders and Swann when they expressed the dedication of the geeks to getting the best quality recordings and playbacks:

This is a song of reproduction.

I had a little gramophone. I'd wind it round and round. And with a sharpish needle. It made a cheerful sound.

And then they amplified it. It was much louder then. And used sharpened fibre needles. To make it soft again.

Today for reproduction. I'm as eager as can be. Count me among the faithful fans. Of high fidelity.

High fidelity,

Hi-Fi's the thing for me.

With an LP disk and an FM set,

And a corner reflex cabinet.

High frequency range,

Complete with auto-change.

All the highest notes neither sharp nor flat,

The ear can't hear as high as that.

Still, I ought to please any passing bat,

With my high fidelity.

The social impact does not need expanding as it is imbedded in the evolution description.

Television – Evolution and Social Impact. The first British television broadcast was made by Baird Television's electromechanical system over the BBC radio transmitter in September 1929. By 1939 they were providing a limited amount of programming five days a week. On August 22, 1932, the BBC launched its own regular service using Baird's 30-line electromechanical system, continuing until September 11, 1935. Then on November 2, 1936 they became the world's first regular high-definition television service. TV broadcasts in London were on the air an average of four hours daily from 1936 to 1939. There were 12,000 to 15,000 receivers. Some sets in restaurants or bars might have 100 viewers for sport events, but the outbreak of the Second World War caused the BBC service to be suspended on September 1, 1939, resuming from Alexandra Palace on June 7, 1946.

The first regular colour broadcasts were not until 1967. Again it was the BBC!

Digital terrestrial television launched in 1998 as a subscription service. Since October 2002, the primary broadcaster is Freeview. Satellite television is dominated by Sky TV subscription service owned by British Sky Broadcasting. It is the provider with the largest number of channels compared to other providers. Freesat is a free satellite service created jointly by the BBC and ITV, it does not need a viewing card. It is the UK's first provider of high definition television without a subscription; one channel was available at launch.

Electromechanical television from:

1926 (Baird mechanical): 30 lines, 5 frame/s, black-and-white experimental transmissions.

1928 experimental colour transmissions.

1932 30 lines, 12.5 frame/s, 3:7 vertical aspect ratio, vertical scanning, ~70x30 pixels per frame, sound, live TV from studio

1936 (Baird): 240 lines, 25 frame/s, line frequency 6000 Hz, used from November 1936 to February 1937. Electronic 1936, EMI took over from Baird using: 405 lines / 50 Hz. This was transmitted by the BBC Alexandra Palace television station initially from November 1936 to 1939 and then 1946 to 1985 (interruption due to 2nd World War).

That is a potted history of the progress made during the century but it is interesting to talk through the progress as seen through my own eyes. Again this will include the social impact.

My first introduction to television was at my uncle's house as I remember in the mid-1950s. I visited to help my cousin with her maths and found that they had just bought an about 9in television (yes- a full nine inches across the screen). This was not a problem as he had also bought a screen shaped magnifying glass at least 15in across to stand in front to enlarge the picture. In his mind it was a success but I found it somewhat unfriendly at the time.

In 1955 I was at another cousin's house when the first Independent Television programme (ITV) was broadcast. Her husband was quite brilliant and he had that day converted his regular television to include receiving transmissions from both BBC and ITV.

In 1957 I was off work for a couple of weeks following an operation and my next door neighbour invited me in each afternoon to watch the Wimbledon tennis with them on their black and white 'tele'. The next year my mother slipped a disc and was laid-up on a door on the single bed in the spare bedroom. The rest of the family clubbed together to rent a 'Radio Rentals' television and put it on top of the wardrobe in her eye line. We thought this would be short term but even after my father died the children had married she was still watching a rented 'tele'. You might well wonder why we did not buy her one as a cheaper option. It was potentially not a cheaper option as the CRT (Cathode Ray Tubes) were inclined to blow up and were extremely costly to replace and you were left without, probably for many weeks. The other point was that as televisions progressed from 30 to 480 then 625 lines by renting you could keep up with the rate of change.

After 1964, television broadcast companies considered developing plasma television as an alternative to televisions using cathode ray tubes. However, LCD (liquid crystal displays) made possible flat-screen television and these, although not as clear as plasma, were cheaper for mass production and it took many years for plasma televisions to became successful. When they finally did it was still not a first choice and new technology was destined to take over.

Colour was introduced at least to Wimbledon in 1967 and Sky TV brought you live test match cricket direct from Australia in the 80s.

In the late 70s our own television was quite up to date and we used it, not only to watch, but we could record programs on to tape to play later and buy or rent tapes of films to watch independently. We could also link video games (fairly primitive and slow compared to the arcades but still acceptable) and add satellite reception for paid transmissions.

Televisions became one of the early electronic devices to be used to keep children quiet during the day and to put them to sleep at night. Not in my opinion one of the significant advances of the century, but the start of something big in the way of hand held games and telephones which seemed to take over from teddy bears and dolls. Socially the whole family benefitted from television but not necessarily as a family. When everyone could have their own choice they seemed to become more individual and more isolated. It appeared that family time became almost non-existent.

Computers – Evolution. Before going onto real computers I will run through some of the ways we handled mathematical problems from early time. The Chinese abacus helped to speed the adding process. The machines that followed did much the same but quicker and maybe created a printed record or retained the results for later use. Even in 1954 when I started work the adding machines that I used had a bank of keyboard numbers which you had to depress and then manually pull a handle to proceed to the next input. It was not long before motor bars were introduced and keyboards were reduced to just the numbers 0 to 9 and with the introduction of small battery operated desk top machines and electronics it was not long before complicated formulae were added to specialised hand held calculators. Shop tills which opened when you pressed down on all the relevant keys were upgraded to electric with exchangeable drawers for one till to be used and managed at a personal level for cash management. Printed receipts were also now available.

The programmable computer was made just before the Second World War and the credit is attributed to either Babbage or Turing. I believe that the variance is down to semantics and that the first electric computer was down to Babbage and the first electronic computer to Turing.

The workings of Colossus did not come into the course I did in 1968 when I learnt all about bits and bytes. IBM, Honeywell, NCR and ICI etc. built computers for commercial use, using a matrix of ferrite rings on crossing wires. From a working point of view these were 8 rings down and 8 rings across. In reality an extra ring was added to each row for a check digit to be created and used as a security check. These matrices were quite small (I seem to remember about three quarters to an inch square) and in England they were assembled in a factory in Croydon (London). I visited these girls working on the conveyer belt where they fed wires through one row of the rings and then passed it on to the next girl for another row. This was amazing to watch and to see the unerring speed at which the production line progressed was an eye-opener. It was also totally outlandish to think that such a primitive manual process was needed to provide the basis of the modern computer. The fastest thing on earth since Wyatt Earp, well! let us just say the fastest calculator ever invented which also had a 'brain' inside it.

The first IBM computer that I was introduced to was a 360/30 and it had 32k bytes of memory (that is 32 times 1056). This used 24k for the booting and operations system, leaving a mere 8k for the programmer to write his program. The machine itself was about four feet wide seven foot deep and five foot high. All the sides could be opened to reveal all the connectors to each ferrite ring and a clever engineer could attach an oscillator and detect faults to the circuitry which happened fairly frequently.

This CPU (Central processing unit) had to be kept in an air conditioned room at a fixed 70 degrees temperature along with the attached disc and tape drives, card reader, console and printers. Yes, the only way to feed information into the mighty machine was typing on the console or using a card reader. In our case we had about 30 girls inputting to card punch machines producing thousands of cards each day. The cards were either from programmers or the daily debit and credit vouchers that would previously have been used for updating the ledgers and statements either manually or using modern cash register machines.

This IBM was originally programmed to allow the processing of the customers and internal accounts through to the monthly balance sheet. The information in the way of statistics particularly was so good that it was not long before us programmers were being ask to provide the different management teams with daily weekly and monthly prints to their specification. This was both exciting and very successful, however, we got to working day and night five and a half days a week. We were told that the computerisation would create a paperless society but after a couple of years I remember ordering 1 million sheets of music score printer paper to be delivered in batches monthly.

I will follow the progress of the office computer later but here I will talk a bit about the other electronic machine that Turing used during the war.

What is generally regarded as the world's first programmable electronic computer (Colossus) was designed and constructed by a Post Office Research Branch team headed by T H Flowers (1905-1998). It was constructed at Dollis Hill, and transported to Bletchley Park near Milton Keynes, where it was demonstrated. Bletchley Park was the centre of British wartime code breaking operations.

The purpose of Colossus was to decipher German non-Morse encrypted communications - known as "Fish" at Bletchley - which were transmitted at high speeds on a teleprinter machine, called the Lorenz SZ, using the Baudot 32 letter alphabet. The mathematician Bill Tute had broken the German teleprinter codes in 1941, but it was recognised that the decryption process could be largely automated to reduce the time taken to decipher the messages. Alan Turing and fellow cryptanalysts had sought technical assistance from the Post Office in the breaking of Enigma.

It is now recognised that without the contribution of the code breaking activity, in which Colossus played a major part, the war may have lasted considerably longer. It was in the preparations for D Day that Colossus proved most valuable, since it was able to track in detail communications between Hitler and his field commanders.

By D Day itself a Colossus Mk II had been built. Flowers had been told that it had to be ready by June 1944 or it would not be of any use. He was not told the reason for the deadline, but realising that it was significant he ensured that the new version was ready for 1st June, five days before D-Day. In fact, there were 11 machines by the end of the War, all but one of which were destroyed on Churchill's orders, the last being moved to GCHQ at Cheltenham where it apparently remained in use until at least 1958 and possibly into the 1960s. A working replica of Colossus has been constructed in recent years and housed at Bletchley Park.

Designed as a code breaking machine, and without an effective memory or a stored program, it was not quite what is regarded as a computer today. Nevertheless, it predated other contenders for the title of the first modern working computer, and was the forerunner of later digital computers.

So in the late 60s we had a small fast computer relying totally on a form of slave labour. Human beings punching holes into what looked like small elongated postcards and then these being hand fed into a mechanical hopper. Assuming that they did not get half eaten and have to be recut, the information was downloaded to a file on a spinning disc. If the reader head touched the face of the disc you had a head crash and lost not just the one file but all the rest of the files already loaded to that disc. This happened too frequently and was usually caused by an impatient operator slowing the disc down by hand instead of letting it stop in its own time. If you got past all the electronic and mechanical steps and managed to write a print file this was sometimes only just the start of a successful run. Printers had a mind of their own and would eat bits of paper for breakfast, lunch and dinner.

This seemed to be the situation with no real belief that computers had or would make life faster and better. The truth was that change happened quicker than anyone could imagine and before long when we attempted to complete our annual five year budget forecast I told my boss that we would be lucky if we could envisage three years ahead let alone five.

Apart from the card input within two years the speed of the transfer of data on the tape and disc drives at least doubled and the printers started running at hundreds of lines a minute. The processing machines were growing at least as quickly and electronic inputting, first through a screen and keyboard typewriter and then through keypads with pre-set functions and numeric keys.

By 1976 each dealer had his own one or two input devices which enabled him to view the market and trade in an instant.

This progress was not limited to the office environment but about that time I visited a factory to see a demonstration of a proposed supermarket till. This would be the start of barcodes on all sales goods so that the item could be scanned and added to the purchases. At this point I feel like the early explorers, like Raleigh when he tried to explain what you should do with the potatoes and tobacco that he brought back from his journeys.

Micro codes on bank cheques, barcodes on retail goods and then postcodes for mail sorting you felt nothing else could be introduced but in an instant we had desktop terminals morphing to desktop computers and then to portable computers. At first this seemed an exaggeration as the first one I took home was almost too heavy for my ten year old boy to lift on to the dining room table.

It was not long before microchips became so small that one the size of your thumbnail held a thousand times the memory of our pride and joy 360/30. Memory by now was not temporary to be transferred and then overwritten with the next process, it could be stored on chip in any selected device.

I particularly remember random access memory (RAM) coming in where you did not have to read it like a book from the beginning but could go directly to specific co-ordinates.

Trying to keep up with myself as I said very early on progress interlocked and overlapped. Television, radio and telephones developed alongside each other and by the end of the century it was predicted that the mobile phone would perform all functions on the one instrument at a higher quality than was available to each separately. We would be able to do banking and pay bills from the phone and cash would become obsolete. I think not in my life time! But what do I know as I have said this many times in the past and been proved wrong.

Computers –Social Impact. I have really only described in a nutshell the evolution of the computer but hope that how completely revolutionary this was, what components were involved, and how quickly it caught and spread has been made clear. I will now try and describe some of the many impacts the computer and its offspring fed into the everyday life of all the age groups.

The whole family were at awe of the changes that came about as a result of computer coding and as I have said the main driver was the developers and the business community. The first major change did come in the supermarkets whth automated tills, where the prices were apparently read from the packaging. This did not seem to be true as you could pay a different price for the same product in different outlets. People thought the goods were packaged specially for each shop but computers were in fact able to read the code and each shop would set a price alongside the code for input to the till. At first we did not trust the machines and they did appear to go wrong quite frequently which left us all in the car park checking our bills before we drove off. It was not long however before we were taking this for granted and thought it might be more accurate than when the butcher appeared to guess a figure and take your cash.

What I knew as a child as 'a penny arcade' was now all driven by technology and apart from the chance to win a teddy bear for your girlfriend you could now play 'computer games' against each other. These were things like 'pac-man' and later 'Nintendo' but all the games were either for two or more people to compete for the highest and at the same time beat the previous highest score on that particular machine, or to compete against each other in forms of table tennis like games. This was all very well but arcades had become expensive and it did not take long before a machine could be bought to plug into the television. These were nowhere near as quick as the arcade but once purchased you could play endless times for endless hours at your or your friend's house. Again it did not seem long before the hand held machines were available and were prevalent in the school playground. Apart from games, music became available on 'walkman' machines which read micro sized tapes and fed sound into earphones. By 1999 something called Bluetooth was brought onto the market and this enabled transmissions direct to headphones and were expected to give hands free operations for telephones and satnavs etc. in cars and to expand facilities in the home.

Alongside these goodies small portable computers were developed, the 'Spectrum' was popular and followed later by the various names like 'Commodore' and then 'Mackintosh' who merged with 'Apple' to become 'Applemac'. It would later again become just 'Apple' and the 'Apple Iphone', with almost all known electronic interfaces planned to be available on the one machine in the early 2000s.

Keeping up with the modern equipment and therefore all your classmates was more than expensive. Some families shared consoles but in practice the value of birthday and Christmas presents went through the roof. I am not sure if the introduction of the Bank Credit Card or price of technology was to blame but, during this period of change, overdrafts, loans and credit, created a buy today pay tomorrow generation.

Mobile Phones deserve a mention in the social impact of computers as they are highly influenced by computerisation. First a little history. The first mention in my working circle was the joke about the smart business traveller who visited Japan and on the way home in the airport lounge he was offered one of these new-fangled devices which was at least as big as a small transistor radio. He thought it would be a talking point at home and bought one. He was about to leave when the salesman pointed out that he had not taken the large accompanying package which he would need (the battery!). When these came on to the market in England they were very popular but not very small. They did contain a battery but because of their size became known as a brick (about the size of a house brick). To work these phones it was necessary to have transmission masts set up and of course there were not many of these across the country. However the phones proved very popular and all walks of life of any age aspired to own one. As I noted earlier by 1999 the phone was all things to all who had one.

Back to the simple computer which after becoming a desktop appliance was rapidly adapted as a home computer. The home computer had most of the office facilities but was as a result of cost constraints rather slower. It did not stop the young and ambitious from loading all the up-to-date technology and the World Wide Web (www) and the internet (Email) so that they could exchange conversations with friends and relatives at home and abroad and interact with business sites. At first this was the preserve of the young but it was actually their grandparents who caught up with them quite quickly before school kids and then parents became efficient. The desktop became a mini computer and then a laptop. As mentioned above all the features of the laptop were destined to be miniaturised and incorporated into the mobile phone.

Also with no fear of repeating myself I believe that computers have changed our lives. Mainly for the good but not always recognised due to the number of government failures in large developments (Linking all doctor surgery records, NHS and Education enhancements etc.) and multiple failures in the communication systems buy the future opportunities are virtually infinite.

I have now covered my main topics in technology and hope that the order and space for each step of progress showed how from the beginning of the century we developed all of the basics for the future development. I do know that as I wrote and read my narratives (not just technololgy) that many asides had either been skimmed over or not included for some reason or another. In the last chapter, before the conclusion, I will address these and hopefully complete the story of the dramatic changes throughout the 20th century and the speed at which they occurred and the significant impact they had on social life.

CHAPTER SIX

MISCELLANY

This was the intended last chapter before the conclusions and is picking out areas for attention which have probably been referenced but also need a greater highlight. I guess that having come this far I must add an additional chapter of Omissions & Afterthoughts just worth a mention.

Education. This has always been a bit of a government pawn and certainly in the latter half of the century teachers must have often wondered why they were not allowed to just get on with teaching the children. The youngest children used to start school at around five or six year olds but pre-school schools were started, not really to help the children or the teachers but to enable the fad (perceived as a need) for mothers to go out to work soon after the birth of a child so that they could pursue a career. Parents organised parent/teacher associations which did not please all heads of schools as the law appeared to give them sole discretion of the management and interpretation of the curriculum. This became a bone of contention when progressive teaching methods were proposed and for example the parents wished to run with the modern methods and traditional teachers did not want change. Government directed but sat on the fence and the unions just did their thing.

That was school up to regular school leaving age but after that in the last quarter of the century most traditional apprenticeships were abolished and National Vocational Qualifications (NVQ's) were introduced. A scheme to fund businesses who employed school leavers over a two year period at £50 per week was also introduced with a view to the employee getting full time, full pay employment. In practice the employee was let go and another youngster taken on. For some supposedly good reason in 1992 polytechnics were reassigned as universities almost doubling the university population. It was also in the 90s that it was a requirement to complete a University degree if you wished to become a nurse. This basically meant that in the future the old system where you could work in a hospital and over several years work up to becoming a Senior Registered Nurse (SRN) and then, maybe, take on a job as matron on a ward of your choice, was a thing of the past. The social impact of these advancements in education were not readily obvious to the man-on-the-street. It would seem that universities would prepare twice as many students to compete for the top jobs and many would finish up no better than having achieved good 'O' or 'A' levels and moved on to meaningful employment. Nurses would be over qualified and lacking in experience which could lead to them only wanting or being capable of going into hospital management and a new lesser paid group of young carers would enter on lower pay working on the wards. Only time will tell!

Leisure. As life changed in the early part of the century, as described in the discussion on transport the leisure activities, it expanded and changed and in the second half of the century we see this going forward. Church, youth club and works outings took on a much more ambitious style. Scouts and guides for instance started summer camps and travelled as far as from London to Cornwall for two weeks under canvas. Works (company) outings started to venture away for evenings or weekends, eating, drinking and dancing. There was a new kind of holiday invented by Butlin's called holiday camps, these provided basic individual accommodation with full board and sporting facilities. You could enter competitions in things like table-tennis, tennis, bowls, netball, darts and snooker or join a day out on a coach trip to a local sight and after all that dance the night away after an after-dinner cabaret. This was the highlight of the year and at first taken as an annual family holiday then as more choices came along the teenagers, families and adult only facilities were introduced. By the late 60s the two week holiday had become two or three weeks and economy air travel hit the market. Foreign package holidays to far flung places like Florida (USA), Greece, Ibiza and possibly Tunis. The Brits and the Germans were the bulk of the travellers and there were notorious fights over bagging places on the beach and around the pools by leaving towels on deckchairs before breakfast. Drinking lager was the evening pastime and the Brits became known as 'lager-louts' particularly on the islands off the Spanish coast. By the end of the century it seemed that all the girls in my office wanted to spend most of their time on the telephone planning their at least two holidays that year and hen and stag nights were not just an evening trip out but a short or less than short holiday to somewhere with guaranteed wall-to-wall sunshine. By this time the invitee was expected to pay their own way (not something I have ever understood). Whether life will return to sanity as my parents would have viewed life only the next century will tell.

Life. Was described by William Shakespeare as the seven ages of man in the 'all the world's a stage speech in 'As you like it'. These divides are still true but would be described differently today. 1, Infancy 2, Schoolboy 3, Teenager 4, Young man 5,

Middle aged 6, Old man 7, Dotage and death. It would have to apply equally to women as men and would need to be politically correct. How with all of life to deal with has anyone found time for innovation? Well not all changes were innovative, planned, they just grew out of change and chance, so let us look at some of the things that the people of the 1900s had to experience.

In the house they went from a tin bath and an outside toilet to all mod cons; bath, shower, sauna, Jacuzzi, with perfumes and oils. Cooking was transformed from coal fires and ranges to gas and electric ovens and hobs with thermostatic controls and Microwave and Induction added for good measure. Heating also benefited from gas and electricity and electric blankets were available for those who did not have central heating. How I actually miss a nice piece of toast done in front of the fire or curling up in clean sheets and blankets (pre-duvets).

Two World Wars intervened and it was not just the young men that went to war it included the middle-aged and as we know many did not return home. Between the wars they suffered the general strike and a recession.

Before the wars the women did not have a vote but after the second war they were fully fledged members of society and along with the vote had worked the land and helped in the munitions factories and assisted in building Spitfires.

Having got this 'independence' they then seemed to choose independence and single mothers became commonly accepted. I do not know of specific links but from Sunday best to posh dance and family outing clothes about the seventies it appeared that even dungarees could pass for formal dress. This, what I consider a definite demise of standards, was only matched by the apparent lack of respect that young school leavers had for others particularly the parents and elderly. This tells me that not all change is for the good.

On the plus side from sharing a house with one of the parents during the first years of marriage and hoping for an increase in wages to be able to afford to rent your own place or best of all being able to get a council house, mortgages and even joint mortgages became available. This came in alongside credit cards and apart from mortgage repayments the monthly capital and interest payments had to be found to pay for the white goods that had become a must with a new house.

Not everyone realised how well off they were at the end of the century as compared to 1900 but one or two examples of accepted modern life compared to the early days can sum up the dramatic changes that had occurred.

In 1946 a professional footballer's wages were capped at £50 per week by 1999 it was up to hundreds of thousands but even amateur players in the sixties and seventies were getting boot money often around the £50 mark.

Imagine a woman with several children standing in front of the fire with one iron in her hand and another one heating on the trivet by the roaring coals (1900) and then no iron at all as all the linen sheets and shirts are non-iron (1999). However between these two events the iron was first electric and then the basic electric steam which was filled with water and then when it had heated up you could release steam to remove creases by pressing a button, but had to be careful not to let it boil dry. Later came the thermostatic control which allowed you to select a delicate or harsh material and you would not either burn or spoil delicate ladies wear. My mother went through all these various innovations.

Cameras also went through many mutations. The Kodak Brownie was the early example of a basic pinhole with a lens which when the shutter was opened for a fixed period (less than a second) light was passed through the project an image onto a piece of sensitive photographic paper. This was on a roll of twelve and had to be sent away to a factory to be processed. A quarter plate camera worked similarly but with a single exposure but also focal and shutter controls. These had to be kept in total darkness until the final picture was printed in a 'dark-room'. In the 1950s I saved my Saturday Morning Errand Boy's money to buy a Coronet Box camera. I went to evening classes to discover how to process film and not only did my own processing in an improvised 'dark-room' but also with a cousin's help built my own enlarger from an old quarter plate camera. Before long I was completely out-of-date endless new cameras came on the market, mainly from Japan. The 35mm was one of the first and this began as a conventional film but proceeded to colour reverse slides which could be projected onto a wall or screen. Instamatic cameras allowed you to take a snap and at the press of a button release the fully processed 2 & a half inch square finished picture. This was followed by digital cameras which could be linked to a computer to produce output either to a screen or a printer. As they were really small and they worked at remarkable speeds (1000ths of a second) you could take as many as you liked onto memory and could view and delete unwanted images before preparing your film slide show. By the end of the century cameras were effectively obsolete as all of this could be done on your camera.

Clothes were expensive and homemade and even in the 60s kids had to wear hand-me-downs but the 1990s was the beginning of the use of foreign cheap labour, either here or abroad and the buy wear once and throwaway society was introduced.

This miscellany has shown mainly physical change but costs of luxury goods particularly in the field of computers and electronics were cheaper than their predecessors relative to income they were also many times better. The youth of 1999 could probably not even envisage how people lived in 1900.

CHAPTER SEVEN

Omissions & Afterthoughts.

I will try to work my way through from 1900 – 1999 with items that, while I was proof reading, I thought should have been included or just came up as an unrelated item but still worthy of note within 20th century innovations.

1900 saw the launch of the first barrage balloon in the U. K. The Zeppelin which was later to be withdrawn after a fatal accident.

1902 the first Teddy Bear named after President 'Teddy' Roosevelt was put on the market.

1913 ladies were freed from corset and lace with the introduction of the Brassiere (Bra). Most men felt it was far too long before the 60s saw women doing away with vests and underskirts.

1935 Scientists discovered Radar as a useful scientific resource.

1938 The art of handwriting was ruined forever with the introduction off the Ballpoint Pen.

The next items are undated as they evolved probably between the two wars.

Water and gas piping which was concrete, steel threaded and sealed with horsehair or lead with leaded joints. These were replaced with copper piping with lead sealing by hand. Later came Yorkshire Joints which were pre-leaded and needed a blowlamp to complete the seal. Step forward and polypiping was the new thing and these joints were a simple snap and clip action. These types of changes gave rise to the start of the do-it-yourself (DIY) era.

Having mentioned piping the other household problem was lighting. Gas lighting was generally superseded by electricity although the house I was bombed out in in 1946 still had some gas lights and the gas lighter still came round to switch the street lights on and off each morning and evening certainly into the fifties. Electric lights were known as tungsten and were temperamental and needed to be replaced frequently. It was understood that they had invented a lifetime filament but would not market it because it would not have been cost effective. Halogen lamps were smaller and designer friendly but although they lasted a lot longer they got very hot. The LED light was similar in most respects to the halogen one but did not get hot and was supposed to last a lifetime. These lights changed the whole concept of Christmas tree lights and you could have many more and not set light to the place. It was goodbye spending hours trying to get last year's lights to work, also no more candles and paper lanterns.

Shoes were usually made of leather or rubber and the soles wore out a lot quicker than the uppers especially with kids kicking balls in school playgrounds and streets. This gave rise to the rubber stick-on sole. Dad's used to put these on new shoes and then hammered metal 'Blakies' onto the back of the heels (even earlier DIY). 1999 and the uppers wore out before the soles.

I mentioned nylon and rayon and when they started to make men's socks with this the early ones never wore out and you had to throw them away when you got fed up with them or they were tatty and did not wash up brightly. This was a far cry from the old woollen sock which was forever being holed at the heel or toe and had to be darned. Darning was fiddly and as mums' did not like doing it they taught their children at an early age that it was their job to darn their own clothes which could include elbows on jumpers.

The last two items are post war and the first results from a lot of the other changes that have gone before and has developed as a result of mainly overseas holidays, immigration and ability to import foreign foods. Yes the eating and drinking that went on at the beginning of the century was mainly at home, in the pub and at the chippy. The Indian immigrants introduced us to curries. This came about when they came over and occupied corner shops and lived over them. We got more than enough all day grocers and I guess someone thought that they could open a takeaway food store. The chaps who had found lager on foreign holidays and got the pubs to sell it then started to try a curry on the way home and this caught on quite suddenly. Other restaurants, particularly Italian and French attracted the now new generation of those who were eating out on a more regular basis. The American burger and chicken eateries also became popular and by 1999 I think every high street appeared to be dominated by 'eat in takeaway places' and charity shops and the good old fashioned chippy lost a lot of its popularity unfortunately except for visits to the seaside.

Albert Arthur Powell MBE (30 January 1900 – 26 June 1982), known as Sandy Powell, was an English comedian best known for his radio work of the 1930s and for his catchphrase 'Can you hear me, mother?'. You must think why have I included this but I felt I must use this to introduce one of the most used and appreciated inventions of the 1900s – the Hearing Aid – which nearly every old man wears, At the beginning of the century all old men seemed to walk with a limp or a walking stick. Not so at the end of the century as a result of medical progress but I still remember the saying as it was so true that everyone had to shout at the older generation. Hearing Aids were able to solve this problem but most of the old men I knew in the 90s did not or would not fit them properly or replace the batteries when needed. It appears that technololgy works but do not trust stubborn old people to necessarily make proper use of it. (QED).

CHAPTER EIGHT

CONCLUSSIONS

I have often been told that I have a good memory and I sometimes like to think that it is true, but I am sure if you have got this far you will be thinking why did he not mention this or that event or invention that to your mind was of much greater impact than some of those included. You will almost certainly not agree with all the interpretations that I have put on political and life effecting changes. I do trust however that you have got as much of a challenge out of reading all the way through as I did writing it.

My own impression from working my way through the 20th century is that for the first half in made a steady natural progress in general terms and that the second half was dynamic. The end result seemed to be that for medication through to transport a timeline was not only possible but necessary whereas when I got to computers, mobile telephones and television things changed so quickly that just writing about all the progress that criss-crossed and overlapped a timeline was really almost impossible and to my mind unnecessary.

As a general summary I think that when my parents were growing up they saw dramatic changes up to the end of the Second World War but most of this to them must have been very traumatic. Two world wars, a general strike and a recession but they still seemed ready to embrace the new world. What they saw was changes to their standards of living and opportunities for their children. The children did not actually know what had hit them but as it grew and developed around they just fell in and accepted it as children. The parents just trusted that their children would be beneficiaries.

These children are the new generation of the 21st century and I just hope they get as much happiness and good health from it as I have from the 20th but I do not think future generations will be the recipients of the same speed of change and the dramatic impacts on life as that which happened in the 1900s.

Printed in Poland
by Amazon Fulfillment
Poland Sp. z o.o., Wrocław

62315622R00166